A Dressage Judge's Handbook

A Dressage Judge's Handbook

With 46 copperplate engravings from
The Training of Horses for School & Battle
by
Johann Elias Ridinger

Kurt Albrecht

J. A. Allen
London

British Library Cataloguing in Publication Data
A catalogue record for this book is available from the
British Library

ISBN 0-85131-459-7

First published in 1981 by Verlag ORAC, Vienna
by J. A. Allen & Co. in 1988
Reprinted 1996

Published in Great Britain by
J. A. Allen & Company Limited
1, Lower Grosvenor Place, Buckingham Palace Road,
London, SW1W 0EL

Printed in Hong Kong by Dah Hua Printing Co. Ltd.
Typeset in Hong Kong by Setrite Typesetters Ltd.

Publisher's Foreword

Johann Elias Ridinger's superb engravings are a valuable complement to Brigadier General Albrecht's
advice to modern dressage judges, serving to remind
us of the original purpose of this most elegant and
beautiful art, and showing in loving detail, highly
trained, supremely athletic horses performing (with
enviable lightness) movements that are as recognizable
and acceptable today as they were in the 18th century.

Presented to an English speaking audience here for
the first time since their publication in 1760, the 46
copperplate engravings are accompanied by explana-
tions which have been faithfully translated from the
old German language by Margarete Harvey. Where
possible these have been left intact, but lack of space
has dictated that some of the more lengthy expositions
be cut. The original German and French captions be-
neath each plate have been left *in situ*.

The Training of Horses for School and Battle — Artist's Preface

Nearly all nations have published works which deal widely with the art of riding and have an incalculable value. Many describe this noble science from the beginning. They deal, for instance, with stud-farming, the raising of foals, their growth and care, as well as their shoeing and management in the stable.

One finds from these works how to choose the type of horse suitable for one's own use, according to their special attributes, characteristics, strength and qualities. One learns what every nation has to recommend to others in the manner of their breaking-in and training, for show as well as in the field. From them one can find out which schools are too high or too low, being more appropriate for the hunt or the campaign, as well as how to recognize illnesses and know the medication or means to guard against them. Everything is so correctly and painstakingly dealt with in these works that there seems nothing more to add, and all these authors are so well known that I would take unnecessary trouble if I named them here.

All enthusiasts can acquire the necessary knowledge of the characteristics and training of horses from the works of many eminent men, and whilst one's own experience should be preferred to science and knowledge gained from books, it is true that our predecessors, through passing on their own experiences, have in many ways smoothed the way for us.

The current masters of the art of riding have made use of published works to give the art the present day perfection we can see. One can convince oneself of this by looking closely at their writings. I would only have to copy that which we already have in abundance if I wanted to add here a complete description of the training of school and war horses.

Therefore, on the advice of friends and enthusiasts, I have decided to use the help of a skilled and experienced person, under whose guidance I have drawn all the lessons from nature, and published them with notes about their application and usage. I believe this work is one of the most detailed ever published and I do not know of another which deals with the subject in this way.

I flatter myself that all lovers of horses will recognize how attentive I have been to please them and how highly I value the honour of being able to recommend my work to their favourable attention.

Augsburg   JOHANN ELIAS RIDINGER
1 May 1760

Biographical Note

Johann Elias Ridinger (1695–1769) studied painting in his home town of Ulm in Germany and from an early age showed a particular interest and aptitude in the representation of animals.

A pupil of Kristoffel Resch, he was often called upon to draw or paint animals caught or killed by the landed gentry and frequently attended hunts himself. He became the official painter to the hunting nobility, depicting his subjects with sympathy and accuracy amidst beautiful landscapes.

Ridinger later established himself in Augsburg, where in 1742 he became Director of the Academy. His two sons were both competent engravers and worked with him. Drawings and engravings were produced in abundance, but Ridinger paintings and the series of 46 copperplate engravings published in his book on the training of riding and war horses in 1760 are extremely rare.

*A Dressage Judge's
Handbook*

Introduction

There are more methods than one of judging dressage tests, but essentially no method is valid unless the judge's knowledge surpasses in all respects the knowledge required of the competitors. Extensive practice of judging can never be a substitute for study; all that it gives is fluency in the expression of knowledge. A really competent judge does not only observe and mark inaccuracies and irregularities; at precisely the same moment he positively recognizes their underlying causes. This of course presupposes years of intelligent and sensitive study of the art, during which he has continuously augmented his fund of knowledge. It is this that enables his mind to grasp instantly the implication of the events which his eyes can only fleetingly observe.

Failing this aptitude, a dressage judge is as unsuited to his function as a school teacher who has only a vague knowledge of the subject upon which he examines his pupils.

If the claim to seniority of a judge is founded only on superior experience of judging, the sole advantage he has over his juniors is greater assurance in the marking of the test sheets. If this be the case, he should at any rate be more generous towards the new recruit to the discipline of dressage than to the seasoned competitor. The former is probably a genuine knowledge seeker who welcomes criticism because he knows that there are gaps in his knowledge which hopefully can be mended, while the latter is usually oblivious of his faults or does not comprehend the real purpose of dressage tests.

Ein bedeckt Pferd mit blenden wie es Zur Schüle geführet wird.
Un cheval couvert avec des lunettes come on le mene au Manege.

A highly strung horse is taught to be led
wearing a blindfold and blankets.

At various times in the past there have been some exceptional horsemen who were not content merely to master the rudiments of the skill of riding; they realized that mastery of the horse had to be based on principles. The fruits of their experiments and observations have been passed on to posterity in their writings; certain laws of horsemanship have been deduced on the basis of their experience and those laws cannot be broken without detriment to the art. It is the duty of present day judges to know them and to ensure respect for them. If they can be so impressed by the flashy movement of extraordinarily powerful horses that they disregard transgressions of principles, they allow the art of dressage to become corrupted.

All aspiring judges of dressage should therefore read and understand the books in which those fundamental principles are exposed. The present manual is intended merely to give some helpful guidelines to judges who esteem dressage as a valuable form of art and wish to guide its practitioners along the right path.

Essential Qualifications for the Judging of Dressage

Fitness to judge dressage does not depend on one factor only.

Proficiency in dressage riding is certainly desirable, but sound and extensive theoretical knowledge is absolutely essential.

The scope and depth of the knowledge required are generally underestimated. Extensive reading is in any case always necessary but not all the books which have been written on the subject are entirely reliable sources of knowledge. A systematic research into the relevant literature will have to be made to select those works that provide the deep understanding that is needed for judging; this vastly surpasses the understanding that is sufficient for enjoyment of the sport. Many years of routine practice of dressage riding cannot absolve one from the necessity of acquiring extensive theoretical knowledge because, although routine practice is needed to develop skill, it does not give the insight essential for judging.

Indeed the objectivity of a judge depends on the extent of his knowledge. Surely it cannot be expected of competitors that they stoically accept time after time erratic and apparently biased judgments which are in fact mostly due to the relative ignorance of some judges.

But whether the more experienced practitioner of the art or the more erudite theoretician makes the better judge is really a moot point. A judge will always be respected if within the short time at his disposal he regularly makes a perspicacious and honest judgment of every performance.

The aspiring judge of dressage will therefore have to appraise without complacency his existing store of knowledge and experience and will devote as much time as is necessary to augment it. He will evidently need extreme enthusiasm and zeal and must find delight in every new acquisition of knowledge. There will of course always be judges who lack this sort of almost fanatical dedication and who do not expect competitors to possess it either. Fortunately they are a minority and it is not for them that this manual has been written, but new dressage judges ought to be deeply impressed by the responsibilities of their position.

One of their responsibilities is to ensure that the sport does not deteriorate into a comparison of equine material in which size and power play the predominant role. Dressage must always remain an inspiration for all riders: purely the art of training a horse to move gracefully, in self-carriage, and to respond instantly to the barely visible indications of its rider.

It must be said that, even in the past, dedicated practitioners of artistic horsemanship were rare in comparison with the great number of riders who had only to obtain the elementary control of their horses necessary for practical purposes. Nevertheless it is this small number that determined the progress of horsemanship through the ages and influenced the important role it has played until fairly recently in the history of mankind.

Nowadays inspired and inspiring masters of horsemanship are even more rare and those that do exist have lost some of the authority that their predecessors enjoyed. The renowned spirit of the breed has been somewhat softened by the present economical necessity of heeding the susceptibilities of the few pupils who can afford superior teaching. Judges therefore have to step into the breach and it is their authority that

Ein Pferd mit dem gürt wie es zur Schule geführet wird.
Un cheval avec la Sangle pour le mener au Manege.

The horse becomes accustomed to wearing
a surcingle in preparation for the
saddle and girth.

will influence for good or bad the state of the art.

One of the purposes of this book is to encourage more devotees of dressage to prepare themselves to become judges. Such a short treatise obviously cannot adequately cover all the important elements of judging but the compactness is deliberate. Genuine enthusiasts will not be satisfied and will be inspired to turn to more extensive texts. As I have already said, a thirst for knowledge is a most important condition of competence to judge. Indeed the task of judging would be tedious were it not for the opportunity it gives for continuously augmenting one's knowledge.

One could say that judges of other equestrian disciplines have received a basic education in dressage judging since all horses have to be schooled to become reliable instruments of human sport.

However, the concepts of equine education in general and of dressage proper are not identical. In fact the term dressage should not be used for novice and elementary tests of submission; it ought to be reserved for performance at Medium to Grand Prix levels of proficiency. Dressage should mean the advanced, special education of some horses with particular aptitudes after completion of the elementary education that all horses should receive.

Therefore to qualify for dressage judging proper, a judge must gain a deep understanding of all the various elements of the advanced, specialized education which he will have to assess during the exercise of his office. In his quest for the extensive knowledge without which he will not be able to justify his appraisal of performance, he must never forget the inviolable fundamental principles; he will often have to refer to the writings of past masters or else seek enlightenment in

9

Das Trottiren von einem jungen Pferd an der Corde.
Le trot d'un jeune Cheval a la longe

Trotting young horses on the lunge is necessary
to teach the *Extended Trot*.

discussions with contemporary experts. Principally he must remember that he has three obligations, namely:

(1) To give guidance to the rider.
(2) To understand perfectly the concepts of dressage.
(3) To have a strong sense of his responsibility for the maintenance in dressage of a high standard of horsemanship.

The good dressage judge does not only estimate correctly the faults which he sees; he is also able to recognize the root cause of incorrectness and to give valuable counsel to the riders. Ideally, he should combine extensive practical experience of dressage riding with superior theoretical knowledge, but some admirable judges have had no riding experience at all. Knowledge however is essential.

Yet neither extensive practical experience nor erudition are enough; considerable alertness is also needed because decisions have to be made in a fraction of a second. Judgment has to be prompt and since it cannot be reversed it has to be based on indisputable knowledge.

A person who is principally attracted to dressage judging by the honour and power which he feels to be attached to the position is as unworthy of his office as one who has not troubled to educate himself properly. Judges are not autocrats; they are merely the servants of the art of horsemanship. They are entitled to respect only if they are able and willing to give sound counsel to the competitors.

In international events, the theoretical knowledge of judges may have been obtained from diverse sources and different interpretations of written texts are pos-

Das Trottiren auf der Volte mit Spanischem Reither u. Sandsack rechts.
Le trot sur la volte avec la machine d'Espagne et le Sac de Sable à la droite

A difficult horse is lunged at the trot with
sandbags and a *"Spanish Rider"*.

12

sible; nevertheless total concensus between judges of different nationalities is essential. There must also be a universally accepted terminology for the notation of observations. The rules drawn up by the FEI ensure this agreement.

Judges dispose of very little time for the wording of observation. Their superior perceptiveness enables them to notice and discern events in a split second but an exact vocabulary must exist for recording observations in terse yet precisely meaningful sentences. It is sometimes believed that unconventionally worded remarks enhance the reputation of a judge and reflect his superior wisdom; this is a mistake. In most cases a few stereotypes are more helpful to the competitors; they are less liable to mystify them than original remarks. If a judge has perfect command of an extensive vocabulary he may be able to make especially telling comments; if he is not exceptionally articulate, it is better that he restrict his choice to the conventional formulas that have a well-known precise meaning.

Judging Carriage and Movement of the Horse

I will discuss to start with the most important elements of a correct performance despite the fact that they are aggregated at the end of the test sheet under the heading "Collective Marks". My reason for giving them priority is that they reflect better than the points for accuracy the quality of the education which the horse has received; after all, this is what the judge is meant to assess. In recent times a form of judging has become established which makes it impossible for a judge to mention apparent shortcomings in a horse's education. It would be highly regrettable if this made him forget that his most important duty remains the correct assessment of the training which has been conducted behind the scene rather than an enumeration of visible flaws in the public performance.

(a) EASE

Ease, that is, absence of excessive tension, is an essential element of correct carriage and movement. A tense horse always responds with irritation, agitation or some other sign of physical or mental resistance to every aid of the rider; this inevitably impairs the correct execution of the movement demanded.

The regularity of the movement and the concordant activity of the trunk and limb muscles (which imparts springiness to the steps) depend on absence of superfluous tension. Moreover if a horse is not sufficiently relaxed, the rider cannot use the aids with subtlety and tact.

Some of the visible indications of ease are the springiness of the steps of the trot (and the consequent smoothness of the ride), the calm oscillations of the tail in accord with the swing of the diagonals, the quiet mobility of the ears, indicating attentiveness to the

Dem Pferd werden die Kugle zum Trottiren angeleget.
L'on met les boules au cheval pour troter.

Balls covered in deerhide tied to the forelegs
are a good remedy for horses who brush
themselves.

rider, and the trust manifested by the boldly opened eyes.

This ease must remain evident even during the execution of a particularly difficult movement.

Ease and elasticity of the steps do not imply submission, what we (Germans) call perviousness to the aids (Durchlassigkeit), but they must be taken into account by the judge when he has to assess the degree of submission of the horse. A tense horse cannot be submissive.

(B) SUBMISSION

Submission is the keystone of impulsion, of straightness, correct carriage and pliability of the hocks. The muscles of the back and trunk of the horse form a plexus related to the muscles of the fore and hind limbs. It is by virtue of this relationship that an aid applied to any part of the thorax is transmitted to all other parts of the horse's body; but if the back muscles are either too taut or too lax they cannot fulfil their co-ordinating role and the trot becomes disunited.

Submission is entirely the result of proper training. The aids become less conspicuous and yet more compelling as it improves. A horse is not submissive if it does not use its back muscles; one of the principal aims of a trainer must therefore be the production of a supple horse – that is of what we (Germans) call a "back mover" in contrast with a "shank mover".

When should points be deducted for insubordination?

(1) For a brief moment a rider can lose control if the horse is startled by some external occurrence; the horse's reaction is a normal reflex and cannot then

be said to constitute an act of disobedience. The important distinction between such a momentary aberration and disobedience resides in the time it takes for the rider to regain control; if he can do so promptly without having to resort to forcible actions the horse's submission should not be questioned.

(2) The horse is tense and obviously irritated by the aids; points should be deducted for insufficient submission.

(3) The horse is calm but is not paying attention to the rider. Inattentiveness is pardonable at the beginning of training and can sometimes be imputed to the ineffectualness of the rider, but, if it is allowed to persist, the chronically inattentive horse makes a fool of a proficient rider also. Indifference to the aids must incur deduction of points on the score of submission.

(c) IMPULSION

Impulsion is at least as important as submission but there are some misconceptions in this respect and a horse with a floating trot is sometimes considered to have great impulsion.

One of the marks of impulsion however is the springiness of the steps but positive and springy forward movement is inconceivable if the hind legs do not engage sufficiently and if the back is inelastic. As has already been said, if the back muscles are inactive, they cannot co-ordinate the movements of the hind and fore legs. The phases of their respective movement must coincide in order to produce graceful and effective forward motion. The complete definition of impulsion should therefore be: desire to go forward, springiness of the steps, suppleness of the back and engagement of the hind limbs.

Impulsion can be directed upward as well as forward, which is why it is often repeated that impulsion and speed are not the same thing.

Submission is a condition of impulsion. If the rider has to use his legs with immoderate force he cannot remain united with his horse. And, vice versa, lack of harmony between the two bodies is detrimental to impulsion.

(D) STRAIGHTNESS

Straightness has always been considered by past masters to be an important condition of effective utilization of the propulsive power of the hindquarters and also of control of equilibrium. No horse is born absolutely straight. Consequently the hind legs do not engage equally in the direction of the centre of gravity. The tendency to move somewhat crookedly is always aggravated at first by the unbalancing effect of the rider; straightness is therefore largely a matter of balance and impulsion. A horse that moves with impulsion stretches both reins with confidence but the tension of the reins must be the result of efficient drive and engagement of the hind limbs and not of a hard pull on the reins by the rider. Impulsion is the important factor and the rider must not attempt to straighten the horse by compressing the convex side of its ribcage with his corresponding leg; both his legs must be used for impulsion.

If a judge notices that a horse is not perfectly straight but that nevertheless it goes with impulsion, stretches the reins lightly but positively and obeys its rider's indications promptly and calmly, he should not attach too much importance to a slight degree of crookedness even if he cannot disregard it entirely.

The judge will have to decide whether he prefers a horse that is straightened by a certain severity of tension – and consequently cannot be moving with ease – or a horse that is not yet absolutely straight but is moving with ease and in self-carriage.

To succeed in straightening a horse by the use of active hands without destroying its calmness and self-carriage demands a degree of skill and knowledge that only very few riders possess.

This is why surrendering the contact (stroking the horse's neck) is such an important action; it clearly reveals whether a horse has regained the equilibrium it enjoyed before it was saddled with the weight of a rider or whether it still needs to find some support in the hand of the rider. In this respect, the "back mover" will always be superior to the "shank mover".

COLLECTION

We can now move on to collection. There are misconceptions on this score also. Many riders, and even some trainers and judges, believe that a horse cannot be collected before it has attained a fairly advanced stage in its education. It is an understandable mistake that arises because the gaits that are said to be collected are too difficult for a horse that has not been gymnastically trained – mentally as well as physically – for a sufficiently long period of time. Still, it is a mistake since it is impossible for a horse to obey any of its rider's indications unless it is able to collect itself in mind and body.

Horses vary in their ability to move collectedly because lengthy training is needed for the develop-

Ein Pferd mit der Spring-Halffter zwischen den Pilliers
Un cheval avec le licou d'entre les Piliers

A horse wears a *Leaping Halter* between
the pillars.

ment of the necessary muscular power. Even so, some degree of gathering of forces, i.e. a certain compression of the anatomical springs of the animal mechanism, is always an essential preparation for every change of speed. A spring, whether it is needed for imparting or regulating motion, or lessening concussion, has to be bent or compressed before it can fulfil its function; this condition applies to any kind of performance, but the degree of compression of springs – or flexion of joints – must be commensurate with the magnitude of the ensuing task.

If the word "shortened" were used instead of "collected" there would be no confusion.

The degree of collection is not determined, as many believe, by the degree of "bridling", but by the degree of flexion of the hind joints. The resilience of these joints has to be developed by training.

The term "bridling" is no longer part of the equestrian vocabulary; many young riders and judges have never heard it, and so it is necessary to explain that a horse is said to bridle when it elevates its neck and draws in its chin. Correct bridling is essential because it allows transmission of the effect of the reins to the hindquarters; so if a horse cannot be bridled, it cannot be collected. Nevertheless it is unfortunate that it is so often said that bridling is the "outward manifestation of intrinsic collection"; this leads many riders to countenance stiffness in the region of the poll in the early stages of training. Stiffness in this region has to be corrected at some stage by appropriate gymnastic work but correction is much more difficult and time consuming if delayed until the horse is strong enough to execute the "collected" gaits.

The readiness of a horse to bridle depends partly on

23

relaxation of the mandibular muscles and partly on the position of the neck. Faults in these respects have to be corrected in the early part of a horse's education if one wants to avoid serious difficulties at a later stage; a horse that does not bridle is an insubordinate horse. There are judges who believe that some stiffness of the poll must be tolerated in novice tests and even maintain that a relatively poked nose is part and parcel of the relaxed body carriage that has to be evident at that stage of a horse's education. They are mistaken, but the reason for their mistake lies in the controversial subject of "flexions of the poll and jaws".

The cause of the argument about flexions of the poll is misunderstanding or misinterpretation of the teachings of some past experts.

It is undeniable that achieving perfect compliance of mouth and poll solely by the practice of the various exercises involving the whole body is a lengthy business and one may have to be content with a result that falls short of perfection for some time. This is why many riders handle the horse's neck and use various rein effects or "flexions" to overcome resistance to bridling, but usually the localized yielding is obtained at the expense of loss of calm and/or freedom of movement. Dressage riding has undeservedly acquired a bad reputation because the unwritten law which states that manipulation of the neck must remain strictly the preserve of undisputed experts is too often infringed. Disagreement between horse and rider is the inevitable consequence of exacting demands; a rider should not risk it before he can be justifiably confident of his ability to overcome every form of resistance.

A horse must be submissive before one can ask it to execute an exercise of a difficulty even slightly in

Das Compliment *vor dem aufsitzen.*
Le Compliment avant que de Monter à cheval.

The *Salute* before mounting is the custom in all
riding schools.

excess of its current level of ability. Submission is always essential but it is very important that the rider has the wisdom to distinguish between perplexity and wilful resistance.

If a horse manifests opposition to its rider's intention during the performance of a test, the judge will have to discern whether the rider is an expert who has not yet achieved his object or a dilettante who resorts to unseemly methods to satisfy unworthy ambitions.

The rider most likely to succeed is the one who, from the beginning of training, concentrates on improving the suppleness of the body of the horse as a whole rather than of one part in isolation.

Similarly, the judge must assess the whole horse, and should not be too pernickety about the position or movement of one isolated part.

There are circumstances behind every satisfactory or unsatisfactory execution of a movement and they are not discernible to a judge who is not exceptionally knowledgeable and perspicacious.

Yet knowledge and perspicacity are the attributes that a judge must have if he is not to remain merely a scorer of faults, incapable of offering useful counsel to the rider. The latter does need a counsellor who understands the root cause of difficulties and knows the proper method of correction.

The improvement of the horse's capacity for collection is an important and continuous process during the whole period of its education. The wrong idea that flexion at the poll is the criterion of collection must lead to faulty judgment. It is therefore apropos to examine now the real origin of collection – i.e. the mechanism of the hind joints.

The unschooled horse utilizes the muscular power

of its hindquarters almost exclusively for propulsion. The hind limbs deliver the considerable force needed to project the heavy body forward at the trot and the canter. Every time a hind foot is set down, the hind joints, though serving almost entirely the production of forward movement, must be bent sufficiently by the weight of the animal to store the force which must produce the next step of the trot or spring of the canter. Movements of the trunk, head and neck also contribute to the production of forward movement.

If the forward movement is to be maintained unimpaired by the weight of a rider, to start with the rider also must move – carefully linking his movements to the movements of the horse – moreover the "springs" (or joints of the hindquarters), have to be compressed more to ensure the effective propulsion of the combined mass by the supporting hind leg.

This coiling of springs, i.e. increased flexion of the hind joints is arduous and a horse normally resists it if the muscles of the hind legs have not been adequately developed by special gymnastic work; with a rider on its back and with relatively unbending hocks, a horse has to swing its hind legs more vigorously or more rapidly to maintain speed. The extreme example of this vigorous swinging of hind limbs is seen in the racing gallop.

As the gymnastic development of the muscles of the hindquarters progresses and the elasticity of the joints improves, their weight carrying capacity increases and eventually speed can be maintained with considerably less to-and-fro swinging of the hind limbs and at the same time the collected gaits also become easier.

Tension of the reins, or contact, means the connection between the rider's hand and the horse's mouth. But there can be a "soft" or a "hard" tension, a "firm" or a "light" tension or again a "loss of contact".

The tension of the reins should not in any case be produced by opposition to forward movement by actively restraining hands; it has to be the result of the co-ordinated hand and leg aids of the rider "containing" or "framing" the body of the horse.

An optimum tension of reins cannot be defined; it has to vary according to speed.

But the judge must know that insufficient or non-existent tension of the reins reveals either improper training, wrong application of the aids or a poor seat.

He cannot remark on its cause but it must influence the collective mark for seat and use of the aids.

CADENCE

Cadence in equitation is a term applied to the trot or the canter but not the walk; the latter can be "well-marked", correct, in four-time or otherwise, but never cadenced.

The trot or the canter can be cadenced only if the horse is perfectly balanced; the slightly prolonged period of suspension which gives the spectator the illusion of greater upward projection of the mass depends on stability of equilibrium.

The rider obviously cannot see the effect of cadence but if he is sitting correctly he can feel the prolonged period of suspension and the more accentuated flexion of hocks which are the distinguishing features of cadence.

A horse that does not engage its hind legs sufficient-

Frey vom boden auszusitzen erster Tempo.
Monter à cheval de la Terre premier temps.

In *Mounting* from the ground, the first stage has
to be easy and calm.

ly has perforce too much weight on the forehand; it cannot be in stable equilibrium and the gait must therefore lack cadence. For example, a Piaffer in which the forelimbs "stick" to the ground and the hind feet are lifted up energetically or swung sideways lacks cadence even if the movements of the limbs are quite rhythmical.

Hence when a judge assesses cadence he simultaneously assesses balance.

In nearly all cases balance and cadence have to be developed by fairly lengthy gymnastic training. Burdened with a rider, very few horses quickly regain their natural equilibrium and the use of their back muscles in the early stages of training.

Furthermore a horse may be well balanced at working trot or canter but find its equilibrium compromised (and cadence lost) at medium trot or canter; it will then start to "run". This a sure indication of inadequate development of the muscular power of the hind limbs.

There are judges who do not attach enough importance to cadence; they fail to understand that a horse that does not show cadence in the extended gaits cannot be in proper balance.

WORK IN POSITION

Correct lateral spinal flexion and work in position are the basis of straightness in all movement on a single track and subsequently of correctness in the movements on two tracks.

Teaching a horse to curve itself uniformly from head to tail in the direction of the movement is a critical part of its education; it does not do this when it moves at liberty. As for everything else, the training

The second stage in *Mounting* is to sit upon
the horse.

has to be progressive. Forcing an insufficiently trained horse to adjust the curvature of its body to the curvature of the track causes it at least considerable discomfort if not actual pain. It is normal that it puts up resistance.

In fact 90 per cent of resistances can be traced back to this unreasonable demand. Only the small remainder can be attributed to temperamental awkwardness. (Many a ewe-neck is created in the early stages of training by the incomprehension of the rider.)

Suppleness varies between individuals but invariably it will be found that it is much more difficult to obtain lateral spinal flexion on one side than on the other.

All horses are born "crooked" and have a convex and a concave side; the convex side is usually called the hard side, the concave side, the soft side. Which is the more difficult is debatable but most riders understand that the more difficult side is the soft side, i.e. the side on which they feel that their hand is empty because the horse evades the contact by turning its neck and hindquarters in that direction.

The hardness of one side cannot be obliterated by determined opposition by the hand to the pull on the rein applied by the horse. At best it can be corrected momentarily but not without causing annoyance. Total obliteration of crookedness is never easy and always requires considerable skill and theoretical knowledge.

"Wrong position" must not only be briefly noted by the judge; it must automatically cause him to deduce some other important fault.

To conclude this consideration of the most important

elements of a correct performance, I have to say that I think that the decision by the FEI to aggregate them and have them marked conjointly at the end of the test almost as an afterthought is regrettable. They are the really significant signs of good training and the factors that give dressage "spectator appeal".

The intention was to prevent judges overlooking the quality of the whole when they had finished appraising the details.

In practise this intention has been frustrated; indeed for a number of reasons it could never have been realized.

For one thing, how can one estimate with a number the value of imponderables like the "purity of the gaits", the "freedom and regularity of the movement", or "impulsion", "animation", "springiness of the steps", "suppleness of the back", "engagement of the hindquarters", or again "submission", "attentiveness and trust", "harmony", "ease of the movement", "fluency", "chewing of the bit", "tension of the reins", "lightness of the forehand" or "position of the rider and correct application of the aids"?

Secondly it makes it impossible for a judge to make a distinction between the factors that can be attributed to the quality of the training and those that are linked to the conformation and special aptitudes of the horse. Yet dressage judging ought to remain principally concerned with the appraisal of training methods. Thirdly, such things as submission, lightness of the forehand, ease of the movements are not identical and should not be aggregated.

Seat of the rider and correct application of the aids are perhaps the most significant signs of good training but it is impossible to give them a numerical value.

Drittes Tempo fest zu sitzen im Sattel samt Zurechtrichtung der Zügel.
Troisième temps pour se Mettre ferme dans la selle et apréter la Bride.

Sitting firmly in the saddle with the reins held
correctly is the third stage of *Mounting*.

34

Finally there is too little time for reflexion and carefully considered grading of the various performances.

For all the above reasons the collective marks introduce an inevitable subjectiveness into the judging of dressage tests.

However, it is not to suggest improvements to the system of judging that I have written this book but rather to help judges to use the system to the best advantage of the competitors. Here are some guidelines:

(1) Certain features that are parcelled under the title "paces", such as, for example, freedom and regularity, can be a peculiarity of the horse or the result of the training methods of the rider.

If a judge feels compelled to point out that the cause of imperfection lies in the rider he can underline the word freedom; the rider is thus told that the mark applies principally to him.

If neither a serious imperfection nor an outstandingly correct performance have to be pointed out the rule is that the collective mark is the average for all the features considered.

(2) The criteria of impulsion have already been explained. However, the word impulsion implies among other things liveliness or "freshness" of the movement. This may mislead riders; the word applies to the movement, not to the horse and it does not mean freshness in the sense of restiveness or hypertension.

In dressage *the important factors of impulsion are the suppleness of the back and the engagement of the hindquarters. If these criteria are not satisfied, marks must be deducted on the score of impulsion.*

35

Hurry, i.e. the running gait of the "shank-mover" is therefore not impulsion and must be marked unfavourably. Here again, underlining the particular element incurring the low mark is helpful to the rider.

(3) The third single collective mark has to apply indiscriminately to various elements of submission, each one of which can be estimated differently depending on personal criteria. The single mark is a meaningless average of the marks the judge mentally awards for each element. He can however underline a particular feature to which he wants to draw the attention of the rider.

A plus or a minus can be marked over a particular element but this is all that the judge has time for.

(4) Similarly rider's seat and position, correctness and effect of the aids are aggregated and make it necessary to average the marks applicable to each part. The problem needs to be considered carefully.

The wording of this section suggests that "Seat and Position" of the rider have to be judged solely from the point of view of appearance and that "Correctness and Effect of the Aids" are something different. *One must however assume that the rider's seat cannot be incorrect if the horse's performance is correct in all important respects.*

To put it differently, the rider's outline may not conform to an ideal but the presentation is nevertheless harmonious. Conversely a rider endowed with natural elegance may appear correct by virtue of his passivity but his presentation lacks charm, spark and quality particularly in the more difficult movements.

36

Die gute Action eines Reuthers zu Pferd.
La belle posture d'un Cavalier à cheval.

This figure shows how the rider should sit on
his horse, elegant and straight.

The judge must not allow himself to be impressed by purely outward appearances. Position, seat, effectiveness have all to be judged in the light of the quality of the entire presentation.

Effectiveness combined with discreetness in the use of the aids naturally deserves to be marked generously. Regrettably it has to be said that many riders have an ineffective seat and counteract its ineffectiveness by inordinate activity of legs and hands.

Their ambition is almost invariably frustrated because no amount of activity of hands and legs can compensate for the incorrectness or ineffectiveness of the seat.

Fair judgment of carriage and gait depends on a proper understanding of all the elements that have been discussed in this chapter.

Judging Gaits and Movements in Tests of Various Standards

A judge, evidently, must know the criteria for the various stages of a horse's education. He may very rarely see a horse that is trained to satisfy entirely the standards of the class in which it is presented, yet the image of a properly educated horse and of correct movement at each level has to be engraved upon his mind. It is not possible to compare performances accurately and quickly unless their quality can be measured against a clearly recognizable standard. A judge who realizes that his most important duty is to help competitors will know the regular process of equine education but his quickness of perception has to be developed and it is for this reason that he is required to judge at novice and elementary level before he can be upgraded and considered suitable to judge advanced dressage.

The development of perception and of the ability to translate knowledge instantly into an accurate notation is a continual process. A good judge is never satisfied with the existing state of his acumen; he cannot rest on his laurels and, just like the good rider, he can never stop learning.

A dressage test (like all other tests of equine adeptness) is intended to demonstrate "what the rider has made of the horse" and the judge must always be able to discern whether the tune is being set by the rider or by the horse; in other words, in a quandary he will have to decide which of the two deserves the better placing: the horse with superior conformation and gaits that makes even an average rider look good, or the obviously less advantaged horse that reveals the skill of its rider by executing the movements of the test with equal ease and accuracy.

At the time of writing the official view inclines towards preference for the latter but there always will

Ein junges Pferd in dem rohen Natürlichen Schritt gerade aus.
Un jeune cheval dans son pas Naturel tout droit.

A young horse must learn to *Walk* calmly on a
straight line in the snaffle bridle.

be borderline cases when the judge will have to make a difficult decision.

The innate impulsion or expressiveness of the movement of some horses is always lost for a while when natural equilibrium is disturbed by the presence of the rider; intelligent and sensitive training is needed to restore it.

Impulsion does not depend only on a horse's natural liveliness; it is also a matter of physical strength. A movement cannot be expressive if the horse lacks the strength needed to perform it with ease. The criteria of impulsion must therefore vary according to the stage of education that is tested.

The tests are classified in increasing order of difficulty;

Stage 1: Novice and Elementary	Tests of the basic education required by all horses before they can be specialized
Stage 2: Medium	
Stage 3: Prix St George, Intermediaire I	
Stage 4: Intermediaire II, Grand Prix and Special	

STAGE I

All horses, regardless of their intended specialization, and even if they are kept for leisure riding rather than competitive sport, should satisfy the requirements for these tests.

During this period of its education the horse must learn to adapt itself to the task of carrying a rider in walk, trot and canter – to go forward willingly on the course prescribed by the rider – and to hold its neck and head in all the three gaits in a suitable position for effective use of the reins for control of speed and direction. At the end of this period the horse should be able to move in horizontal equilibrium and to adjust its spinal curve to the curvature of large circles and of the (well-rounded) corners of the school.

Exercises for which definite control of the hind-quarters is needed, such as half-pirouettes, are not required because they cannot be executed correctly by the majority of novice horses.

In the transitional period before the next stage, the horse has to learn to rein-back correctly.

When it has completed this basic education and is out of novice classes, the horse must satisfy the following requirements of elementary tests:

At the trot
Moderate but perceptible cadence, resulting from regular two-time movement in diagonals and elasticity of the steps.

Freely maintained head position characteristic of horizontal equilibrium – the nose approaching the vertical – indicating that the parotid glands have retreated and are no longer painfully compressed by the posterior rami of the mandible.

A convexity of the upper border of the neck – due to proper development of the dorsal neck muscles and atrophy of the ventral ones – which ensures that the rein effects extend "through" the body to the hind-quarters.

A moderate elevation of the neck (an imaginary horizontal line must pass through the corners of the mouth and the hip joint).

43

In the corners of the arena and on all curves of the track the horse must be curved around the rider's inside leg to enable the hind feet to step in the traces of the fore feet; otherwise the hindquarters would deviate outwards and the inside fore would become over-loaded.

The back must have attained a degree of elasticity sufficient to allow the rider to sit to the movement and maintain his balance easily.

In the medium trot, the carrying capacity of the hindquarters must have been developed sufficiently to permit the longer phase of suspension that allows an energetic to-and-fro swinging of the diagonals; in other words the horse must not hurry when it feels the rider tensing his loin and closing his legs to order the change of speed.

At this stage, in the medium trot the horse must be allowed some balancing assistance in the form of a relatively firmer tension of reins.

The canter
The horse must have learned to execute the transition to canter in both directions upon the indication of the aids and exactly at the point specified. This proves that it has been taught to understand the aids and to obey them instantly. Moreover, the joints of the hindquarters, and particularly the hocks, must have become resilient enough to allow the horse to spring immediately into canter on command since the outside hind alone has to support the mass and thrust it forward for the first spring. To this end the collecting aids (i.e. half-halts) have to permeate the entire mass to reach the hocks and again this is possible only if the head and neck position are correct.

If a horse still needs momentum to get into canter, and speed to continue cantering, it shows that it has not yet got the strength to preserve horizontal equilibrium. The rein effects are then only hand actions without the collecting effect of correct half-halts. It also shows that the rider does not know how to use his legs to control the hindquarters.

Pronounced flexion of hocks cannot be demanded of a horse in the first stages of its education; only the working and medium canter are required in the novice and elementary tests because flexion of hocks is essential for the extended canter to prevent it deteriorating into a four-time run.

Simple changes of canter directly through the walk would overtax the hind joints at this period of training. They demand greater development of the muscles of the hind legs and greater elasticity of the hocks than can be expected; hence in the simple changes some intervening steps of the trot are always required.

The walk

In novice and elementary tests the walk is exclusively a medium walk.

The quality of the walk gives important information about the state of balance of the horse. It is impossible to attach too much importance to the correctness of the walk, which must be exactly in four-time.

In a four-time walk the horse has to balance itself – and for one moment one of the legs on the ground is carrying more weight than the others. If it cannot do so, or rather if it has lost this normal ability under the influence of the rider (one of the principal causes of an incorrect walk is an incorrect seat), its walk will de-

Der Schulgerechte Schritt an der Wand gerade aus.
Le pas du Manege à coté de la Muraille tout droit.

Schooling the horse alongside the wall at
the *Walk* makes him move straight
and carry his head well.

teriorate into a jog or an amble. Moreover, the walk has to flow, meaning that the rider should not have to constantly urge the horse on with imperious legs. The impulsion must come from the normal driving effect of a good seat. If the rider sits up easily, without stiffening his hip and leg joints, his pelvic movements cause each hind leg alternately to engage so that it can support the mass for a sufficiently long period of time. If the four-time beat remains constant it shows that the hindquarters are strong enough to carry the weight of the rider; on the contrary, if the rider is too heavy or sits too heavily, considering the actual strength of the hindquarters, each hind foot has to be set down hurriedly.

A horse may have had a good four-time walk with long strides before it was ever ridden and have lost this special attribute at the beginning of its training. A knowledgeable and alert rider will soon restore the walk to its original correctness. Unfortunately an innately inefficient walking technique can never be transformed by the rider, however competent he may be.

For the medium walk, the driving and supporting functions of the hindquarters have to be equally balanced. It would be wrong to include in the tests the half-pirouettes which demand greater muscular power of the hindquarters than can be expected at this stage.

Stage 2
The transition from Stage 1 to Stage 2 cannot happen overnight. A lengthy period of gymnastic training is always needed before the more difficult movements can be executed correctly. How lengthy must depend

47

partly on the physical and mental aptitudes of the horse and partly on the extent of the rider's knowledge and skill. Aptitudes are so variable that the length of the period of gymnastic preparation needed in each case cannot be defined, but the rider must understand the nature of the difficulties that make rapid progress difficult.

The hasty rider will always be made to regret his impatience. His horse may resist his unreasonable demands with violence or for the sake of peace, may execute the movement required in a manner that protects it against pain. But it will not be a correct execution and if nonetheless this satisfies the rider, he will find it all the more difficult to obtain correctness at a later stage. He may even find it impossible; the correction of established faults is always extremely difficult and can be carried out successfully only by an expert.

Incorrectness that reveals serious disagreement in the course of training must be marked more severely than brief opposition to the rider's will and must be remarked upon by the judge, if possible in the test sheet or else in conversation with the rider.

The weight bearing capacity of the hindquarters has to be improved by gymnastic exercises of very progressive difficulty which will increase the strength and elasticity of muscles and joints. The result should be more expressive cadence and improvement in self-carriage. The changes of tempo at the trot and the canter become progressively easier, deterioration of equilibrium and rhythm gradually less frequent.

Changes of tempo (the lengthening or shortening of steps) cannot be correctly executed before a horse can be gathered or let out without this causing it to alter in any way the timing of the movement.

Der Schulgerechte Trab an der Corde auf der Volte rechts.
Le trot ou Manege à la corde sur la Volte à la droite.

Lungeing at the *Trot* is the foundation of all
subsequent schooling; it frees the shoulders
and supples the quarters.

The conformation of a horse may preclude spectacular extension; if the timing remains unchanged and the cadence well-marked the movement should be noted as favourably as the extension of the better endowed animal. *In case of doubt, the judge has to discern whether he has before him a rider capable of bringing out all the talent of the horse – or a rider who is content to accept the most that the horse is actually willing to offer.*

A horse presented in tests of the second stage of training must have been brought to a degree of submission that permits the fine interplay of hands and legs called co-ordination of aids.

It is this co-ordination of aids that enables the rider to "engage the hindquarters" (compress their springs) and obtain the degree of gathering which ensures stability in the transitions from one gait to the other and in the changes of tempo. Impulsion can now be utilized to impart more springiness and more cadence to the movements, instead of serving exclusively the production of forward motion.

The simple changes of canter must now be executed directly through the walk, and the half-pirouettes have to be correctly performed.

Equal lateral flexibility to both the right and the left must be established and the poll must have become supple enough to ensure a stable, submissive head carriage in all movements. This being the case, there should be no lateral tilting of the head, no deviation of the hindquarters in the corners of the arena or on the curvatures of the track. The horse must curve its body unresistingly round the inside leg of the rider and must stretch equally the inside positioning rein and the outside regulating and tactfully collecting rein. Resistance in the above respects indicates callous disregard during

Der Schulrechte Trab an der Wand gerade aus.
Le trot du Manege à la Muraille tout droit.

Schooling at the *Trot* alongside the wall
improves the action of the horse
and the firm position of
the rider.

training of an awkward conformation of the mandible and compression of the parotid glands by its posterior rami.

When all resistances to flexion have been eradicated the horse is ready to be ridden in a double bridle.

The Curb Bit

At the time of writing all tests of medium standard and above have to be ridden in a simple double bridle with the reins in both hands. (Rules have varied from time to time and in different countries.) Very few modern riders are taught the old and perfectly correct cavalry way of holding the reins, that is both curb reins in one hand, but the bridoon reins separated. In itself, the present day customary 2:2 division of the reins is not wrong but riders ought to understand that it imposes perfect stillness of the hands; the curb rein must never be used for giving direction and position. If in the course of training one may sometimes have to "bend the horse forcibly" it is absolutely essential to put the curb rein out of action for the moment and to use only the bridoon rein. It follows that if one rides with a curb rein in each hand, it is almost entirely with seat and legs that the horse has to be directed since the curb rein should not be used for this purpose except to give the barest indication of change of position.

The real function of the curb is to facilitate collection. Riders who customarily use it for steering soon deaden the bars of the mouth so much so that increasingly vigorous hand actions become necessary to control speed or direction until finally the horse is quite ungovernable . . .

Backward stepping (the "rein-back") will have been practised in a more or less correct form in the course of

Changiren im Schritt auf der Volte rechts.
Le changement au pas sur la Volte à la droite.

Teaching the horse to turn quickly on the *Volte*
when asked makes him agile and amenable.

the basic education of the horse, but at the present stage a considerable degree of submission is required. The transition to the rein-back requires efficient engagement of the hindquarters and submission of the hocks, and a correct rein-back is proof of the harmoniously integrated activity of the most important parts of the horse's body: head, neck, shoulders, back and hindquarters.

Stiffness or stiffening of any of them makes the correct execution of the rein-back quite impossible.

The first condition of correctness, apart from engagement of the hind legs, is the perfect relaxation of the mandibular and neck muscles, enabling a head and neck position that permits the rein aids to act on the joints of the hindquarters.

Before indicating backward stepping, the rider has to ensure collection at the halt. The necessity for correct leg aids at the halt prior to the rein-back is not appreciated by all riders but is nonetheless very important. However, the rider must have very good reflexes for it is only too easy to cause an improperly prepared and premature backward movement by the horse.

It is only when the horse is physically and mentally collected that the leg and hand aids can become more insistent and set the horse in movement.

In the earlier stages of training a horse will commence the rein-back by first displacing one hind leg and then the diagonally opposite fore leg. As training progresses, the very short interval of time between the movements of fore and hind limbs is gradually shortened until the displacement of the diagonally opposite limbs gives the "appearance" of complete simultaneity.

It would be quite wrong to mark this apparently complete simultaneity as incorrect.

At the same moment as the feet are lifted up, the mass of the body has to recede but there must be absolutely no change in the head and neck position.

The reins therefore must not be shortened; the aids have to be understood only by the horse; for the spectator they must remain invisible.

This does not mean that perfect discreetness in the use of the aids is possible in the course of training but discreetness nonetheless is the aim and it should be achieved as soon as possible.

The rider must use his legs as well as his hands to determine the rein-back but again he has to be very aware of his reactions in order to avoid a "yielding to the leg", i.e. any lateral displacement of the hindquarters.

As with all other things, a correct seat is supremely important. The rider may minimally incline his body forward at the commencement of the movement, but during its execution he must remain perfectly upright and avoid any change of position which would unavoidably disturb the horse's poise.

Hastiness in the execution of the rein-back, a widening of the placing of the hind feet, a "getting behind the bit" are all serious faults that prove that the rider is ignorant of the criteria of a correct rein-back. The faults should be attributed to the rider rather than to the horse, but it is unfortunately impractical to point this out in the testsheet . . .

The counter-canter is already required in elementary tests; nevertheless a horse that cannot yet easily maintain in true canter the stable head and neck carriage that denotes horizontal equilibrium should never be asked to counter-canter.

Gallopp auf den hancken gerade aus lincks.
Le galop sur la hanche à la gauche sur la ligne.

The *Canter* will develop more easily from a
well-established trot, and just as the
trot is the basis of schooling on
the ground, the canter is the
basis of movements
above the ground.

To preserve stable equilibrium in the canter, the muscular strength of the hind legs must have been sufficiently developed to permit a slight delay in the extension of the hock during the propelling phase of the movement. This relatively prolonged flexion of the hock enables the rider to lengthen and shorten the springs of the canter without compromising horizontal equilibrium and agitating the horse.

Impulsion has to be maintained by consecutive, more or less accentuated and yet soft pressures of the rider's (lower) legs at the girth in rhythm with the movement.

Unquiet hands and exaggerated body movements disturb the horse's equilibrium and are detrimental to calm and to the fluentness of the movement.

But it is the seat again that has the most important function in the collected canter.

Only a good seat enables the rider to feel and foster the engagement of the horse's hind legs in the direction of the centre of gravity. If the joints of the hind legs are flexed as they come into support they take over some of the weight which is borne by the fore legs in the natural canter; the forehand is thus considerably lightened. The result is a rocking movement which allows constant adhesion of the rider's buttocks to the saddle. Excessive swinging of relatively unbending hind legs make it well nigh impossible for the rider to go with the movement.

A rider who sits up with supple loins and keeps his lower legs in constant contact with the horse's sides helps the horse to canter straight by setting both hind legs under its body. This is one of the most important conditions of further progress in the horse's education.

A correct seat is even more important at the counter-canter. The perfect poise of the rider is essential to the preservation of the delicate equilibrium of the horse. Faulty alignment of hind and fore feet, faulty head and neck position are indications of the disturbing seat of the rider.

A rider who thinks that the reins alone can impose upon the horse an appropriate position in the counter-canter will find out once more that they cannot compensate for a badly balanced seat.

Wrong distribution of the rider's weight, even if it does not always force the horse to change or break its canter, at least gives it permission to do so. This is why a correct counter-canter is such an important touchstone of the correctness of the horse and of the rider.

The simple, immediate change of canter after only one stride at the walk can never be fluent and therefore correct before the horse's submission to the aids of hands and legs is perfect. The simple change is intended to demonstrate the degree of submission to the half-halts.

It has already been explained that the simple change (canter-walk-canter) requires a considerable development of the strength of the muscles involved in the flexion of the hocks. But apart from this, a horse cannot be expected to execute the transition fluently if the rider neglects to use his seat and legs to prepare it by guiding the hind legs and causing them to be set down further forward. If only the hands are used for the halt the horse will throw its mass against the bit and brake with the fore legs or else it will disregard the rider's command. Again the rider has himself to blame for the disobedience of the horse. More than one intervening stride of the walk should incur less deduction of marks than those blatant signs of insubordination.

The half-pirouette is also a good yardstick of the degree of submission to be expected at this level.

If it has to be executed from the halt, a thinking rider will prepare the movement beforehand with a half-halt to get the hind feet to step well forward and put the horse in position to execute the movement easily.

If he has neglected to do so, he will have to collect the horse at the halt with spurs and hands, a delicate procedure requiring considerable feel and very good reflexes. It is intended to make the horse alert to the oncoming aids but most horses become excited when asked to "concentrate their forces" in this manner. If one has to collect at the halt, two things are essential: firstly the horse must have been carefully trained to understand what is required, and secondly, the rider has to be extremely skilful and knowledgeable.

The half-pirouette is not an easy exercise; it cannot be executed correctly unless greater impulsion is available; but to produce the extra impulsion required, an enhanced degree of collection has to be obtained.

Backward stepping or failure to continue stepping in correct four-time shows not only that the horse has not got enough impulsion, but also that the rider is still unable to control the hindquarters.

On the other hand, a hasty execution of the movement points either to precarious equilibrium (which again may be the fault of the rider) or to insufficient development of the muscular strength of the hind legs.

If the inside hind foot remains rooted to the ground, it is usually because the inside leg of the rider is insufficiently active.

The criteria of correctness are therefore: unaltered

Relevirter Galopp lincks gerade aus auf den halben hancken.
Le galop relevé à la gauche sur la ligne à la demie hanche.

The *Collected Canter* is more elevated and
better for hunting and falconry as the horse
canters in a shortened stride.

carriage of the horse throughout the execution of the movement, maintenance of four-time movement, and distinct steps of the inside hind foot; these are the signs of satisfactory impulsion as well as proof of stability and of the carrying aptitude of the hindquarters.

If the half-pirouette has to be executed while continuing to walk, the same criteria have to be used, and it is also essential to ensure sufficient impulsion by achieving a greater degree of collection at the walk before starting the turn.

Again this demands considerable skill on the part of the rider; while trying to obtain the enhanced collection needed, he has to avoid disrupting the four-time sequence of the walk or bringing the horse to a standstill.

The distinguishing features of the half-pirouette from the halt, and the half-pirouette while walking is that in the second case increased collection has to be achieved by shortening the steps of the walk, while in the first case it is obtained by intensifying the horse's desire to go forward without allowing it to move.

However, the actual execution of the half-pirouette has to be judged by the same standards: during the turn the movement must be fluent and the four-time sequence of the walk must be preserved.

In the transition from collected walk to half-pirouette and half-pirouette to collected walk there must be no discontinuity of movement; the rider must therefore be able to regulate the exact degree of collection needed at each moment.

But this is not an aptitude restricted to dressage riding; show-jumping riders must be able to educate their horses to the same degree of submission to the aids. This demands great self-discipline, intelligence and patience on the part of the rider; nevertheless a rider who just practises "free jumping of obstacles with a rider aboard" will always have to accept the fact that his results in competition depend on the mood of his horse and on chance. Unfortunately, chance in show-jumping does not always favour the better rider.

Judges of show-jumping cannot counsel the rider; their objectivity is unquestionable because faults are easily counted, but the rider is left to draw his own conclusions after a disappointing performance and he does not always make the right inferences.

Yet judging show-jumping gives one an excellent opportunity to test and augment one's existing knowledge and improve one's acumen. With sufficient practice one can also acquire the perspicaciousness that enables the prompt assessment of a rider's horsemanship.

STAGE 3

Now we have come to tests of specialized, advanced dressage education. It has to be pointed out that the further progress of the horse's education depends on the further progress of the rider's horsemanship; it is preferable that he should have reached the required level of competence before undertaking the demanding training of the horse. The ideal is to find a good dressage trainer who can provide a veteran equine "school master". If the rider is less expert than the horse, the latter's progress must inevitably be arrested ... if it does not recede.

The movements that have to be assessed at this stage are the flying changes (eventually at every stride if the horse is very talented) and all the movements on two tracks. The elevation of the forehand and the supple-

Changiren im Galop rechts auf der Volte.
Le changement au Galop sur la Volte à la droit.

A horse that is fluent at the _Volte_ is more
useful in a campaign.

ness of the hocks must have been developed to a sufficient degree and any trace of stiffness of neck and back muscles eradicated.

Considerably greater engagement of the hocks is required and should cause the horse neither discomfort, nor pain nor agitation.

The judge must be capable of correctly assessing every manifestation of agitation, and understanding its cause.

He can infer numerous shortcomings from such manifestations for which marks have to be deducted – and should not hesitate to decide on a very low mark in appropriate circumstances.

At this stage of a horse's education, the dressage judge's task is quite difficult; on the one hand, he has to observe and mark a fairly long series of movements; on the other hand, he must constantly look out for deviations from the overall standards of correctness.

Judges of dressage must therefore take advantage of every opportunity that can help them to develop their perceptiveness, but their discernment of what is correct or incorrect depends on their knowledge of proper standards.

Errors of judgment or even apparent errors are inevitable if only one member of a body of judges has a conception of correctness at variance with the official orthodox view. If unanimity of views is complete, disparate appreciations can only – at least in theory – be explained by the different vantage points of the judges.

The absolute necessity of total concensus between judges regarding criteria of correctness must be constantly stressed.

It would be reasonable to expect judges to meet regularly between competitions – at least at national level – to discuss possible different conceptions of standards. These discussions must be as exhaustive as needed to prevent any accusation of dictatorial exer-

Parade im Gallopp rechts.
La Parade au galop à la droite.

The Halt from the canter happens through a
tightening of the reins and an
unexaggerated resistance in
the back and torso.

cise of authority by any member of the panel. They must serve to clarify doubtful points and broaden the knowledge of all judges attending the forum.

Certain "classical principles" have remained unchanged over the course of some centuries; it is indeed impossible to change them since they are the foundation of what can validly be called horsemanship.

Principles are invariable. There are however other rules that have been frequently changed or modified, as for example those concerning the design of saddles and bits; furthermore methods of training and even the conception of the ideal outline of a trained horse have varied at times and in different countries.

Of course no national federation can afford to be insular in its outlook and rules; yet each federation may have a preference for certain training methods and present its riders with practical, intelligible, generally valid guide lines regarding the training of horses.

It should not be forgotten either that some procedures are applicable to all horses but, since horses are individuals, methods have to be sufficiently flexible to accommodate differences of physique and temperament. The idea that only one method is acceptable, purely on the ground that it is the one most generally practised, inevitably produces disappointing results. On the other hand, contravening of basic principles, due either to perverseness or ignorance of their significance, inevitably also makes for fiasco.

Contraventions of this kind have to be censured by judges even if their admonitions are not well received by the riders concerned.

We can now examine the special requirements of Stage 3.

The flying change of canter is a movement that any untrained, unmounted horse does quite naturally. It may execute the change more neatly and with greater facility to one side than to the other but the action does not perturb it at all. It is only when the rider "puts a finger in the works", by commanding the change with legs, seat and hands, that the horse may get excited.

One of the first things one is taught when learning to ride is that a horse cannot obey the actions of legs, hands and seat, called aids, before it has learnt to understand their meaning and cannot obey the aids promptly if it is not able to do so.

Submission depends on a number of physical and psychological factors.

A detailed enumeration of physical disadvantages would exceed the scope of this book; temperamental difficulties are even more numerous. One thing however can be stated positively: any disturbance of the normal calmness of a horse is a sign of psychological perturbation, no matter whether the cause is bodily inaptitude or mental confusion. This is something that we should not forget, especially when teaching a horse to execute repeated flying changes.

Horses endowed by nature with a good sense of balance quickly recover their innate equilibrium when they have to adjust to the load of a rider; such horses are least likely to be disturbed by the flying change.

Even in the canter, they distribute the load so perfectly on hind and fore limbs that they are never induced to avoid overloading a weaker hind leg by moving crookedly, bending the wrong way and generally grudging active forward movement. They feel secure and therefore do not become agitated.

They should be able to execute the change of lead in

Der Schulrechte Paſs an der Wand.
Le pas l'amble du Manege à la muraille.

The horse schooled to *Pace* can be a very
comfortable ride and is favoured by noble
ladies for riding out.

the air calmly and fluently without loss of impulsion
and without deviation of the croup if:

(1) Their obedience to the aids is confirmed.
(2) If right and left lateral curvature have become
    equally easy.

Provided that the rider does not confuse it with
wrongly timed aids or unbalance it with untidy body
movement, a talented horse will experience little difficulty in learning to execute the repeated changes.

Still, even a talented horse may find changes of lead
difficult if it has been made to do them before its hind
legs have become sufficiently strong; it will then need
to balance the weight on both hind legs simultaneously instead of the inside one alone and the hindquarters
will then deviate from the straight track.

It will also hesitate, lose impulsion before the
change and will then spring sideways rather than forwards.

Once a horse has discovered the knack of stabilizing
itself in this manner in preparation for the flying
change, it is extremely difficult, if at all possible, to
teach it to execute the change correctly at a later stage
when its hindquarters have acquired the necessary
strength. The sideways springing or the deviation of
the croup will persist and this is nearly always a sign
that a highly talented horse has been made to execute
the movement prematurely.

In contrast with the above deviation, a lifting of the
croup indicates that a horse has not yet learnt to flex
the hocks and hence cannot set down its inside hind
sufficiently forward to support on its own the weight
of the body.

In this case, the suppleness of the hocks has to be developed by appropriate gymnastic work before the flying changes can be practised.

Greater difficulty of execution of the change to one side, or refusal to change behind to this side, is an indication of insufficient elasticity of the opposite side of the body.

It is pointless then to continue practising flying changes before lateral suppleness of both sides has been obtained by appropriate exercises; resistance to lateral curvature by the mandibular muscles is particularly detrimental to the correct execution of flying changes.

But it is not with strength of legs and arms that one overcomes those resistances.

The rider cannot be effective if he has a wrong conception of the nature of the "aids" and does not comprehend the reason of their effectiveness. Correct application of the aids does not mean vigorous use of arms and legs. The first duty of the judge is to assess the correctness of the horse in the flying changes; nevertheless he cannot disregard completely the actions of the rider.

His opinion of these will have to be expressed at the end of the test sheet, in the column for rider's position and seat, correctness and effect of the aids.

The *lateral movements* were originally purely a means to an end; nowadays they are an end in themselves and are included in tests. Thus the judge can influence the education of the horse in an indirect way by appraising the manner of execution of these movements, since it is only if they are correctly performed that they can fulfil their original purpose.

Evidently the judge himself must be aware of the

purpose of the lateral movements if he is not to be impressed purely by acrobatic ability.

His appraisal has naturally got to be measured against a standard of excellence; but he must also be able to determine whether the shortcomings of a particular horse are attributable to its inherent limitations or to the inexpertness of the rider. The judge cannot express his opinion in the marks for the movement but he can and must do so in the marks for seat and aids.

It should never be forgotten that dressage tests are principally intended to appreciate the skill of the trainer and this should always be properly estimated in the test sheet.

For many riders it is the movement known as "yielding to the leg" that introduces the horse to the lateral movements. Nevertheless "yielding to the leg" is not classified as a lateral movement because its main purpose is to teach the horse to understand the significance of the predominant aid of one leg. But obedience to the leg is only one of several factors of correct execution of the lateral movements.

In principle a horse should not be made to "yield to the leg" at any other gait than the walk.

Once the exercise has fulfilled its principal function (which is to teach the horse to obey the indication of one leg behind the girth) it can be largely excluded in subsequent training although there are cases, which I do not intend to discuss, when it can be resorted to again to overcome a particularly stubborn resistance to lateral inflexion.

The most important criteria of all the lateral movements are correct position and inflexion.

Position and inflexion have their own respective function but they also have a common one, which is to

71

Das Zurückgehen an der Wand.
Le reculement à la muraille.

Where a horse can neither go forward nor turn
around one is obliged to go backwards.
Reining Back is an important
exercise; without it, the
horse is not properly
trained.

curve the horse uniformly from head to tail for the purpose of facilitating control of speed.

The special functions of the *shoulder-in* are firstly to develop the pliancy of mouth, poll, ribcage and hocks and the freedom of movement of the shoulders in preparation for the execution of voltes and other tight turns; and secondly to develop the horse's agility so that it can displace itself sideways without treading on its own feet or otherwise endangering its balance.

The shoulder-in is certainly one of the most useful exercises for the promotion of all those aims, but it is also one of the most difficult to execute correctly.

It is rarely demanded in tests because it should properly be regarded as a means to an end instead of an end in itself.

There are two ways of executing a shoulder-in. In the one, the shoulders are moved well inside the track and four hoof traces are visible; in the other, inside hind and outside fore are on the track and trace one line. But the important criteria of correctness are:

(1) The horse must be uniformly flexed to the inside from head to tail rather than bent at the withers;
(2) The head must be correctly positioned: ears on the same horizontal plane and nose close to the vertical; the beat must remain unaltered;
(3) The shoulders have to be moved in; the shoulder-in is not a "croup out" movement.

The shoulder-in fulfils its originally intended function only if it measures up to those three conditions.

It is normally executed at the trot, though the walk is used to teach the horse to understand the movement.

The shoulder-in at the canter, also called "Plie", is rarely used.

The *Travers* is intended to perfect flexion and position and also to make the horse more attentive to the leg aids.

In a correctly executed Travers, outside hind and inside fore provide the drive; inside hind and outside fore safeguard balance. (If the inside fore is overloaded, causing the outside fore to step over it, either because the neck is bent more than the ribcage or because the croup is turned in too much, the exercise is useless.)

The Travers is always executed as a "half-travers", that is as a more or less oblique forward movement rather than a purely lateral movement. It is then called half-pass or traversale, done either from one end of the arena to the diagonally opposite end, or from the centre line to the track, or vice versa, or on the centre line, or again in zig-zag fashion.

The travers can also be performed as a "croup inward" movement, either on the long side of the school or on the circle. In this form it is frequently and very properly used as a schooling movement.

The criteria of correctness are proper position and maintenance of the beat.

Forward-sideways movement with lateral curvature in the direction of the movement is not a natural mode of progression for a horse, and it will always resist efforts to put it in this awkward position – or at most will consent for only a few steps – if lateral flexion at the poll continues to cause it some discomfort. It is certainly impossible to enforce the position by the aid of the hands alone.

If the croup precedes the shoulders, the beat is im-

Traverſiren an einer Wand rechts :-
Le Travers à la muraille à la droite

Travers parallel to the wall is advantageous for
the cavalry when they have to close ranks
and maintain a front against the enemy.

paired, the shoulders are restricted, the overloaded inside fore cannot contribute as it must to the forward drive. Even if the test requires that the horse remain parallel to the long side of the arena, this must not imply that the croup must be perfectly in line with the shoulders – let alone precede them. The shoulders must always precede the croup by one half-step.

The travers is executed at walk, trot and canter. It has to be stressed that a correct execution of the movement is impossible if the rider does not sit "on the inside hind", or if he tips forward and overloads the inside fore. A correct seat is of paramount importance. Both legs preserve impulsion while the reins must first indicate the direction and then help the horse to preserve correct position and inflexion during the execution of the movement.

The horse must remain in self-carriage as in movement on one track; this implies a light, steady contact of the reins.

The same criteria apply to the renvers. Incurvation, position and role of the limbs are exactly the same as in the travers, the only difference residing in the positioning of the forehand instead of the hindquarters inside the track.

Lateral movements are difficult only if a horse has not received the rational gymnastic training leading up to them. In reality none of the lateral movements on its own can be considered as a panacea; each one is only part of a systematic programme of development of agility.

However the general attitude of a horse at this level of achievement differs from the one of a horse that has completed its education to Stage 2. This is due to the fact that the Stage 3 horse should be able to perform all the movements in self-carriage. It is self-carriage that

Traverſirt auf der Volte gegẽ der Saüle mit dem Kopf ein ü: der Crouppe aiswærts
Le Travers sur la Volte contre le Pilier avec la tête et la croupe en dehors.

Travers around the pillar with the head in and the
croup out supples the shoulders and improves
control of the quarters.

enables the movements to be performed with sufficient ease; it is also self-carriage that imparts elegance to those movements.

Cadence also depends on self-carriage. It can never be shown by a horse that has not developed sufficient strength of the hindquarters and suppleness of the hocks to move in horizontal equilibrium and comply readily with the rider's aids for increased loading of the hindquarters and consequent lightening of the fore legs and elevation of the forehand.

As a result of self-carriage the rider appears to have more horse "in front and less behind". A further advantage of self-carriage is that it allows the rider to use the aids more sparingly and yet with greater effect.

At this stage of training the reins should have no more than a "collecting function" or at most indicate the rider's intentions. They cannot be used for steering; this function is now devolved entirely to seat and legs. Should the judge notice that the rider attempts to manoeuver the horse with his hands, he will have to conclude that either the rider lacks knowledge or that the horse is not adequately prepared for the test.

At medium level, the double bridle is often compulsory. In principle, the rider ought to hold one bridoon rein in one hand, curb reins and the other bridoon rein in the other hand though there is no rule forbidding the holding of the reins in the 2:2 fashion (left bridoon and curb rein in the left hand, right bridoon and curb rein in the right hand). Few judges nowadays infer any reason for adoption of one manner or the other. In principle an accomplished horse should be as easily rideable with the reins arranged in the 2:2, 3:1 fashion or even on the curb alone without a bridoon (the bridoon being a concession to the clumsiness of the cavalry trooper or the necessities of campaign riding).

Traverſiren mit der Grouppe gegen der Säule auf einem engē Creiſe rechts.
Le Travers la croupe contre le Pilier sur un petit cercle à la droite .

Travers with the quarters around the pillar teaches
the horse to turn on the spot.

The important thing is that the rider should perfectly comprehend the function of the curb bit.

The foremost requirement that must be met before the horse can be fully bitted is a degree of submission to all the aids permitting control by tactful actions; eventually the actions of hands, legs and seat should become so unobtrusive that they can be perceived only with difficulty by the spectator although they are very tangible for the horse and for all their politeness have become potent means of communication of the rider's intentions.

The charm of a presentation will always depend on a refined concordance of the aids.

Obtrusive use of any one set of aids indicates insufficient pliancy of poll, neck, back or hocks which should preclude the use of the curb.

All the exercises designed to develop the pliancy of every one of those parts are better conducted with the horse bitted in a snaffle. The effect of the curb is so wholly collecting that its use for the purpose of decreasing resistance to incurvation or position is difficult and inadvisable because it can be detrimental to the soundness and sensitivity of the bars of the mouth.

Since the 2:2 division of the reins has become customary in all tests in which the double bridle is prescribed, many riders have been misled into making up for the deficiencies of training by using the curb to impose lateral flexion. A judge should always keenly watch out for this fault and somehow point it out to the rider.

Canter pirouettes are included nowadays in some tests which are not up to the level of Stage 4; this is understandable since most horses presented in tests of Stage 3 are being trained with the view of being presented eventually in tests of Grand Prix level.

Traverſiren auf der Volte im weiten Kreiſe linets.
Le Travers sur la Volte sur un cercle large à la gauche.

Travers on the large circle allows the horse
more freedom in the exercise.

Nevertheless it has to be pointed out, especially to judges, that the step from Stage 3 to Stage 4 is a very big one; the aptitudes required of horses presented in tests of Stage 3 level of difficulty need not be as outstanding as those which are absolutely essential if one contemplates presenting a horse in the next stage.

To start with, there is the matter of conformation. Croup high, short-backed, long-legged horses, with insufficiently angulated hind limbs – to name only some disadvantages – will almost certainly never make the grade and if a rider nevertheless wishes to take part in competitions at the highest level of difficulty, he will have to put up with an "insufficient" note for many of the movements and impose upon the judges the obligation of pointing out the unsuitability of the animal.

Even if a horse has been regularly well-marked in Prix St George it does not follow that it will cut an honourable figure in the more advanced tests.

Rider and judge must be able to appraise correctly any limiting factor of conformation; there are more than enough other conditions of suitability – and not least, the competence of the rider.

All the movements or "schools" which in the past only a "school horse" had to be capable of executing are now included in presentations at Stage 4; canter pirouettes, passage and piaffer.

Dressage and Training

When selecting a horse specifically for dressage and planning a training programme, one must always bear in mind that hope of success at the highest level of proficiency is a delusion if the horse does not possess a variety of favourable inbred qualities.

Suitable conformation, as has already been said, is essential, but it is not the only important attribute; intelligence, boldness and amenability are equally necessary.

We must not forget either the rider element, the skill and knowledge required to exploit the qualities of the horse.

To attain the summit in dressage, a rider has to be intelligent and mature; in addition he must have enormous powers of empathy. It is this last attribute in particular that enables the gifted rider to breathe a stirring artistic quality into a merely technically correct presentation.

A horse presented in Stage 4 tests has to be a "school horse". The term is old-fashioned and its meaning is unknown nowadays to many judges and many riders. It does not indicate a horse used for teaching purposes in riding schools and riding academies. It used to be applied to horses trained to perform certain so-called Airs of the Manege (the school walk, the piaffer, the passage, the flying changes and the canter pirouettes), capable of adjusting the curvature of their body to the curvature of circles of a small diameter (voltes) and of halting instantly "on the haunches" (in total submission to the aids of hands and legs combined). Since these terms are no longer part of the vocabulary of the FEI they have fallen into oblivion.

Nevertheless the concepts are not outdated and were well expressed in those terms; they described an

Traverſiren links auf einem Creiſe von Länge des Pferds.
Le Travers à la gauche sur un cercle la longueur du cheval.

Travers to the left on a circle the length of the
horse is like turning on a plate, causing the
horse to use its hindquarters more
to free the forehand.

advanced degree of schooling and a precise level of proficiency in the execution of various difficult movements called "movements of the low or the high school". I feel therefore that judges of dressage ought to know the exact meaning of those words because, to do justice to riders and horses, they ought to appreciate the disparity of aims and standards of excellence relevant to Stages 3 and 4.

If a rider presents a horse in considerably more severe tests of agility than the Prix St George, purely on the strength of some success at this latter level and without appreciating the very superior qualities required – such as supreme submission, perfect self-carriage, exceptional muscular power and exceptional elasticity of hind joints – logically it is he the rider who ought to be impugned rather than the unfortunate animal that is probably being physically and mentally overtaxed.

Unfortunately, judges have to mark in the only way open to them; the prescribed formula restricts them to criticism of the horse rather than the rider; and so it is not unusual to find an excellent, even exceptionally accomplished horse disparagingly judged because the rider is incapable of bringing forth its outstanding virtues.

To facilitate comparison and understanding, the different requirements are set out here side by side:

The Campaign Horse (Stages 1, 2 and 3 inclusive)	The School Horse Specialized dressage (Stage 4), piaffer, passage, changes, pirouettes)

POSITION AFTER THE HALT

When both hind feet have stepped under the centre of gravity, a slight forward step of the fore feet must be permitted. It is impossible for the horse to remain at a standstill with deeply flexed hocks for any length of time. If the forward stepping of the fore feet is not allowed, the horse must step backward behind, a much more serious fault

The School Horse has been subjected to a lengthy process of gymnastic training that enables it to remain at a halt with pronouncedly flexed hocks for a few seconds and also to accept a more stringent rein aid

RESUMPTION OF FORWARD MOVEMENT

After the halt in stable equilibrium, the rider's legs give the impulse for the forward movement (transition from halt to collected or medium walk)

In the case of the School Horse, the tension of reins has remained constant during the halt and it is with his hands that the rider lightens the forehand coverting the school halt with very engaged hind legs into forward movement. This is due to the rebound of the hind leg "springs" after their compression (school walk)

TRANSITION TO TROT

Firmer use of seat aid (the rider drawing himself taller while straightening his lumbar spine by decreasing pelvic inclination) together with diagonal but not completely simultaneous effect of hands and lower legs (but not heels or spurs).

(Working, collected or medium trot)

An adroit combination of the same aids in quicker succession and with more emphasis should produce the cadenced school trot (characterized by greater impulsion) which can be transformed into passage or piaffer by judicious opposition by the hand to forward propulsion

TRANSITION TO CANTER

Transition to canter is commanded by the combined aids of legs and hands; the promptness of execution by the horse depends on the degree of readiness, i.e. submission attained. (Working, collected or medium canter)

In the case of the School Horse a firmer tension of reins in the direction of the outside hind induces the springy forward movement characteristic of the school canter. The school canter is a prerequisite for the canter pirouette

TRANSITION TO STANDSTILL

Even a well-trained campaign horse needs to be prepared for the halt by more pronounced pressures of the rider's lower legs, inducing the

In the school parade, (direct transition to halt of a School horse) the hands act first; this however presupposes the stepping of the hind feet

hind feet to tread further forward. The relatively prolonged opposition by the inside hand to the propulsive action of the outside hind stops the forward movement	directly under the centre of gravity and deep flexion of hocks

The difference between so-called campaign horses and school horses resides only in the degree of aptitude for a special task.

Aptitude is conditioned by a multiplicity of factors, namely conformation, angulation of joints, alertness, character, temperament of the horse . . . and also competence of the rider. It is obviously the responsibility of the rider to decide whether those conditions are favourable enough to justify hopes of satisfactory results at the highest level of difficulty.

Yet it is also the duty of a judge to express his personal opinion if he recognizes obvious disparities between aims and aptitudes.

Even if all the special difficulties pertaining to the tests of extreme proficiency are not always included in a particular test, a horse cannot be described as a Grand Prix subject before it has been thoroughly trained to perform all movements with ease.

At this point it is necessary to go into greater detail regarding correct execution of particular movements – and requisite aptitudes – because these are the movements that riders find especially complicated and that aspiring judges of advanced dressage have so little occasion to observe. However, to start with, it has to be stressed that the movements are not in themselves particularly complicated provided that riders and

Der Schluß auf einer halben Volte im Traverſirē das Pferd auf die Haucte geſezt.
Le Travers serré sur la demie Volte en mettant le cheval sur la hanche.

The result of *Travers* on a half volte with the
croup to the wall is very beautiful and can be
performed at revues and festivals to show
the skill of the rider.

horses possess the necessary aptitudes. Inability to execute them correctly must always be imputed to inaptitude of horse or rider in some respect.

THE PIAFFER

The definition of the piaffer in the *Austrian Manual of Dressage* is clear: the piaffer is a movement on the spot in which the sequence and beat of the steps must be the same as in the passage; the horse, with pronouncedly flexed hocks, being distinctly set on the hindquarters which must carry the greater portion of the total weight.

This definition evidently implies that a horse is not ready for piaffer before its hindquarters are strong enough to allow the hindfeet to step under the common centre of gravity, thus relieving the forehand of all but a small proportion of the weight.

Deficiency in this respect can be ascribed to a number of causes:

(a) a real weakness of conformation – as, for example, meagre and/or insufficiently angulated hindlimbs, a prominent croup, too long or too weak a back – which no amount of gymnastic work can entirely neutralize;

(b) insufficient gymnastic training of the muscles of the hind legs for their arduous role in the flexion of the hocks;

(c) lack of knowledge on the part of the rider (causing him to muddle collection and flexion of the poll and to rely more on the effect of severe application of legs, spurs and whip than on a rational and systematic programme of training);

(d) or simply the rider's unawareness of the relevant criteria.

The words "on the spot" are particularly significant. At each step about two-thirds of the combined horse and rider weight has to be taken off a fore leg diagonal and transferred to the rear supporting hind leg. This obviously entails a considerable development of the supportive power of the hind legs which were designed by nature to function much more as levers for serving forward movement than as flexible props.

To allow the movement to be executed on the spot, each time one hind foot is detached from the ground, the other one has to balance the weight and this necessitates a momentarily greater flexion of the hock.

If the supportive and propulsive forces of the hind legs are exactly balanced or, worse, if the propulsive force remains even slightly dominant, the horse cannot be "set on the hindquarters" with well flexed hocks.

The criteria are the same for the passage. Besides the shortcomings already mentioned, that prevent a horse from executing the piaffer correctly (deficient aptitude or deficient training), certain flaws in the passage can be due either to:

(a) unsuitable training method;
(b) premature practice of the movement.

Flaws can be extremely difficult to redress if they are left uncorrected even for a short time.

A notable example of an unsuitable training method is the preparation of the passage by work in hand when insufficient regard is given to a horse's preparedness; a rider who is not capable of discerning the actual state of equilibrium of the animal (that is whether it carries itself in horizontal equilibrium or with too much

Redopp mit der Hand lincks.
Le Redop à la muraille sur la gauche.

In the *Redop* to the wall, the forehand advances
the quarters a little. When done with more
speed the horse can travers from one side to
the other, right and left.

weight in front, or whether it is already capable of setting itself on the haunches), and yet proceeds with work in hand, in the misconceived belief that the "aid" of the whip can produce the engagement of the hind-quarters, risks obtaining the following results:

(a) a lifting up of the croup by the stiffened, insuf-ficiently engaged hind legs, especially facilitated by the overloading of the fore legs;
(b) a swaying of the hindquarters.

Both evasions represent an escape valve which the horse will always resort to when it has discovered its convenience, even after the supportive capacity of its hindquarters has been satisfactorily developed.

Untimely training in hand to obtain a piaffer will produce similar evasions. Every rider should realize how painful the flexion of the hocks is during the supportive phase of the movement if the involved muscles have not been intelligently and considerately developed for this unwonted activity. Forced by an artificial aid to feign a piaffer or passage, a horse some-times lifts up the unloaded hind foot with considerable energy but without sufficiently flexing all the joints of the loaded hind limb. This results in a lifting up of the croup on the same side. There are many riders who are eminently satisfied by this kind of deception and, re-grettably, some judges also. It is however a very se-rious fault which automatically entails another equally serious one: the useless activity of the hind limbs throws extra weight onto the forehand, causing a stac-cato action of the fore legs ... The genuine piaffer is a very elegant movement; the counterfeit piaffer is on

Redopp auf der Volte linEks im weiten Creise.
Le Redop sur la Volte à la gauche sur un cercle large

Redop on a large circle on the volte is a fast turn
useful when before a battalion or in a duel. It
also prevents the enemy getting behind.

the contrary totally graceless and should be firmly condemned.

Yet this is not the only harmful consequence of untimely stimulation of the movement from the ground. It can also impair the realization of the main object of dressage training, i.e. the gradual modification of the initial manner of going of the young or untrained mounted horse (with the major part of the total weight on the forehand), culminating in a reversal of the balance (with the hindquarters supporting a larger proportion of the load). This requires a long period of systematic gymnastic training. If the process is shortened or neglected, the aim is unlikely to be achieved and the rider must then lose all prospect of producing a school horse, capable of performing a passage with sufficient elevation of the forehand and a marked period of suspension. Nor will the horse ever be able to complete a proper canter pirouette in self-carriage.

THE PASSAGE

The natural passage of a horse is a sort of trotting gait shown often by youngsters, usually stallions, rarely mares or geldings. It then seems to be a manifestation of innate "bossiness" though it can happen also when a horse is subject to some other exciting influence.

Because the gait is not uncommon in youngsters, some riders misguidedly attempt to produce a passage in the early stages of training. After all it does not seem to require any superior development of muscular power. Nevertheless the assumption is wrong.

In this "natural passage" (as this gait of young horses could perhaps be described) it is excitement that produces the muscular tension which has to be de-

Redopp auf einem kleinen Circül von Länge des Pferds rechts.
Redop sur un cercle etroit la longueur du cheval a la droite

Redop to the right on a small circle the length of
the horse, haunches in.

veloped in the dressage horse (by definition a mentally poised animal) by collection; but although there is a period of suspension in the "natural passage", there is very little flexion of the hind joints.

With the added weight of a rider, the pseudo-passage with stiffened hocks soon loses its loftiness and the periods of suspension become shorter and shorter.

As has already been said, *the school passage must never be attempted before the strength of the hind leg muscles has been properly developed.*

Premature practice of the gait is not only detrimental to the soundness of the lower joints; it also has adverse psychological consequences. The considerable stressing of the fetlock joints causes discomfort and possibly pain, hence undesirable agitation and at least an unclean movement, at worst an enduring aversion for the movement. A horse will always be loath to execute a command once it has discovered that obedience is punished by pain.

On the other hand, should the horse have sufficient muscular power, and the rider the ability to impress his intentions on the mind of the animal, a good number of those horses selected for very advanced dressage should be able to learn the passage easily. Nevertheless the expressiveness of the fully developed "school" passage will still depend on a variety of factors – principally inherited physical and psychological advantages.

Here again I quote from the *Austrian Manual of Dressage*: "The passage is an extremely collected trot, with springy well-rounded, rather short steps."

Now if that were the complete definition, any well-balanced horse would be capable of performing a pas-

Pefade oder erhebter Redop auf der halben Volte links.
La Peſſade ou le Redop sur la demie Volte à la gauche.

The *Pasade*, or elevated *Redop*, to the left
on a half volte.

sage . . . However the movement must conform to a further condition: ". . . in the sequence of the trot, with powerful expansion of the springs of the hind legs, and with a long period of suspension, so that the forearms are elevated to the horizontal." This is not so easily achieved. In fact the correct execution of a school passage is not possible before the horse has undergone long and thorough gymnastic training.

A long period of suspension of one diagonal pair of legs is possible only if the combined weight of horse and rider can be balanced for an appreciable length of time on the other diagonal, the supporting pair. For this purpose the supporting hind leg has to step on a spot very close to the line of gravity and this in turn is possible only if it is capable of a sufficient flexion of hock.

But in the passage the role of the grounded hind leg is not as entirely supportive as it is in the piaffer; a fairly equal balance between supportive and propulsive function has to be maintained. Hence for the passage the horse must not "set itself too much on the hind-quarters". The amount of weight transferred to the hind leg must not be so great as to hamper the propulsive action which has to send the mass forward at the next moment.

The supportive force produces the marked elevation; and equal propulsive force must remain available for the powerful forward movement. Any crossing or lateral positioning of the hind legs would of course considerably undermine this force.

Flexion of the hocks can be obtained with greater facility from horses that are higher in front than behind because of very angulated hind legs but they have greater difficulty in the passage than so-called horizontally balanced horses. Their centre of gravity is situated further back and thus more effort is needed to produce forward propulsion.

Therefore the belief that the horse must always be taught the piaffer before the passage is not entirely well-founded.

In any case the passage is an extremely demanding movement which must never be started early. Urging a horse to project the great weight of its own body plus the weight of the rider upward and forward before the hind legs have developed all the necessary power is a sure way of destroying its calm – to the point of frenzy sometimes – and thus inevitably of spoiling the regularity of the beat.

It is also inadvisable to demand at the beginning anything more than the "soft passage" which has a relatively small elevation; the resilience of the hocks has to be patiently developed before perfect equilibrium between the supportive and propulsive forces can be established.

Disregard of any of those conditions of correct execution of the passage is the cause of either major faults or minor flaws which the judge must be able to appreciate and mark according to their importance:

(a) the insufficiently trained joints of the hind legs, incapable of supporting the weight, push and do not carry. The hind legs fail to step sufficiently forward and are only languidly picked up;

(b) the insufficiently developed supportive capacity of the hind legs causes the horse to step wide behind. The overloaded fore legs may sometimes cross instead of moving in a straight line;

(c) a generally flat movement, with barely noticeable lifting of the forearms, insufficient forward stepping of the hind legs and an imperceptible period of suspension. Mostly due to negligent training and premature practice of the movement.

To conclude this discussion of piaffer and passage, and give physical substance to theoretical notions, I will now try to give, I hope, a sufficiently graphic account of the course of the movements.

A properly prepared horse, with good development of hind leg muscular power, moving in a normal state of collection, steps behind close enough to the line of gravity to allow it to execute the transition to piaffer without any loss of composure.

During the execution of the piaffer, rather than moving the hind legs further forward, the horse – with its back well arched and with deeply flexed hind joints – displaces its trunk rearward until the buttocks are behind the hocks. This automatically restricts the field of force of the hind legs and precludes any up and down movement of the croup (which must remain absolutely level), because the backward setting of the body permits only forward movement.

An unmistakable sign of correct activity of the hindquarters and absence of resistance is the perfect steadiness of back and croup. The movement must proceed downward from the hip joint.

A horse that sets itself particularly deeply behind (by displacing its trunk rearward to such an extent that the point of the buttocks comes well behind the point of the hocks) can go into passage only by first "opening" the joints of its haunches (hip and stifle) and then pushing its body forward. The weight is then distri-

Courbette rechts gerade aus von einem Hufschlag.
La Courbette à la droite sur la ligne.

Courbettes, where the horse remains on one spot and raises its forehand, will earn horse and rider high acclaim.

buted equally on the forehand and the hindquarters.

The suitable amount of backward displacement of the centre of gravity depends on the athletic condition attained by the horse as a result of intensive gymnastic training. The nearer the line of gravity approaches the grounded hind foot, the longer becomes the distance that has to be travelled by the croup at the moment of the transition from piaffer to passage and the more the compressed hind joints have to flex. The prolonged engagement of the joints of the supporting hind leg allows a correspondingly long suspension of the un-loaded diagonal pair, but the subsequent simultaneous extension of stifle and hock which has to propel the mass upwards and forwards requires tremendous muscular force.

If the passage has been developed from the piaffer too early, i.e. before the hind joints have been made sufficiently resilient by patient, sensible gymnastic work, the transition from piaffer to passage will lack fluency ... or the piaffer itself will become flawed.

I hope that I have clearly explained why a horse has to be extraordinarily athletic if it is to succeed in making the transition from a piaffer with extreme rear-ward shifting of the trunk without first making a movement that redistributes the weight over hind and fore legs equally. A flowing transition into passage from a piaffer with so much backward displacement of the centre of gravity is an extraordinary tour de force which very few horses can ever achieve to perfection.

THE CANTER PIROUETTE

The canter pirouette also requires great robustness and it is imprudent as well as inconsiderate to start teaching it to a horse before the resilience of its hind joints is sufficiently developed. Imprudent because a horse quickly discovers deceitful ways of protecting itself against unreasonable demands and is always loath to change those ways later when it has become physically capable of executing the movement correctly.

The canter pirouette is developed from the "school canter" which is in fact a four-time canter, though the unassisted human eye is too slow to recognize it as such. In the four-time school canter, the inside hind is grounded a fraction of a moment before the outside fore. We must not however confuse this gait with the totally incorrect four-time "ground scraping" slow (rotary instead of diagonal) canter in which the inside hind steps out of line a fraction of a moment "too late", i.e. after the outside fore.

Nevertheless the pirouette shows more impulsion if the illusion of a three-time canter is preserved. The shorter the interval of time between the steps of outside and inside hind (sometimes amounting to complete simultaneity of the steps) the less correct the pirouette.

There are other criteria of correctness:

— The horse must step with the inside hind on as small a circle as possible.

It is of course principally on the outside hind that maintenance of the canter depends but the size of the circle is measured by the length of the path marked by the inside hind.

When the movement is introduced into the programme of education it may be desirable to let the horse canter on a somewhat bigger circle than for a pirouette proper, but one has to take into account the fact that the forehand has always got to

Courbette gerade aus an der Wand links.
La Courbette à la muraille

The *Courbette* alongside the wall.

describe a greater circumference than the hind legs.

— At each bound of the canter the fore legs must be lightly and gracefully picked up.

A horse that "goes on the forehand" cannot satisfy this latter condition; it just throws the loaded forehand around the hindquarters. This is a very common fault.

However there is another fault caused also by weakness of the hind legs; the trunk can be retracted so far backward over the stiffened joints that it is impossible for the horse to develop impulsion except by hopping on both hind legs.

— A "full pirouette" must consist of six to eight canter springs.

A smaller number clearly signifies loss of impulsion. Now the horse must always have enough impulsion to stop pirouetting at any moment and immediately resume a forward going canter.

The "half-pirouette" must consist of never less than three bounds.

During the execution of the pirouette the horse must clearly be in self-carriage.

This means that it must not attempt to lean on the hand and that the rider must not appear to "lift the forehand up" by force.

A horse that moves with too much weight on the forehand will always take some support on the hand of the rider; conversely a rider who does not know how to use his seat and legs to help the horse to engage its hind legs and preserve the impulsion necessary for self-carriage will always rely too much on his hands.

The criteria of correctness that have just been

enumerated imply that schooling for the pirouette can begin when:

(a) the horse has learnt to flex its hocks;
(b) the muscles controlling the flexion and extension of the hind joints are strong enough to allow the necessary flexion of the hocks;
(c) the poll has become perfectly pliant;
(d) the horse can remain easily in self-carriage;
(e) the rider knows the criteria of correctness of the pirouette;
(f) the rider has acquired the requisite knowledge and skill.

The following are the faults that are commonly seen:

— Not on a "saucer" (the circle described by the inside hind is too large).
— Turning around centre (hindquarters moving around to the same extent as forehand).
— Croup out (hindquarters describing a larger circle than forehand).
— Hopping on both hind feet.
— On the forehand (the rein tension is too strong and the horse throws itself into the turn).
— Rider "lifting" the horse.
— Rider learning backward (excessive bracing of the small of the back destroying the regularity of the beat. The four-time beat is too obvious).

Each fault must incur a loss of marks. But the judge should be more than just a scorer of points.

His theoretical knowledge must enable him to rec-

Halb lüstig rechts gerade aus.
A demi allegre sur la ligne.

One can recognize in *Half Lightness*, a greatly
devoted collection, how well the horse has
been trained.

ognize immediately the basic cause of the faults observed *because he must always be prepared to defend his judgment against any possible adverse criticism.*

At the time of promotion to list 1 (recommended to judge tests of advanced standard), a judge must already possess the solid knowledge that he will need during the exercise of the function to enable him to make positive and incontrovertible decisions. The vagaries of a particular judge are quickly noticed and in the short run cause him to be distrusted by the riders but in the long run the reputation of all judges must suffer from the unreliability of one of their fellows.

ONE–TIME CHANGES
To start with a prevalent misconception must be dispelled: the flying change of canter is a test of submission already demanded in tests of medium standard. But the changes in series at every third or second stride or the one–time changes are *not* a particularly significant criterion of proficiency at the highest level of schooling.

However they are demanded nowadays in the difficult tests of Stage 4.

In fact the one-time changes were introduced into FEI tests of advanced dressage at a fairly late stage. There was indeed a time when they were called "canter-passes" and were frowned upon. However they are now firmly installed into Intermediaire II, the Grand Prix and its equivalent, the Special.

They do of course require a high degree of submission and attention on the part of the horse; they do not however require any special advantage of conformation.

On the contrary, a well-developed pliability of the

Von der Erden zur Erden.
Terre à Terre.

Ground to Ground is a type of canter where the
horse holds itself on the quarters making
little progress.

hind joints can be disadvantageous when the repeated flying changes are first introduced into the schooling programme.

The reason for this is that a correct flying change, in which the hind legs of the horse must engage in the direction of its fore legs, is often strenuous and sometimes painful if the animal is not yet sufficiently robust and supple; it will then instinctively resort to avoidance of stress by turning its hindquarters inwards.

If the rider disregards this evasion and does not immediately take it as a warning to somewhat reduce his exigency, the horse's initial, understandable avoidance of pain quickly becomes an habitual dodge.

Moreover the canter itself usually becomes "scraping", less ground covering, "rounded" and lively.

Horses with rather stiff hind joints at the beginning of their training can more easily oppose their rider's collecting aids and are thus less likely to suffer. Since it is impossible to force them during this very important stage of their training to slow their canter appreciably for more than short moments, their hind legs have more room to swing and therefore can follow in the traces of the fore legs with less difficulty.

However, the flying changes in series, whether three-, two- or one-time, cannot be started before all resistance to inflexion has been eradicated and before the horse has been educated to respond immediately to discreet co-ordinated aids. Otherwise the obtrusive indications of the rider will once again compromise balance, pliancy, position and straightness.

Marking the Test Sheet

The purpose of this primer is not to give the rider detailed guide lines for the training of his horse but rather to give important points of reference for the judging of tests. The preceding chapters were devoted to the special technical requirements of dressage, that is of dressage considered as a particular form of equestrian activity, and as much has been said in this regard that could be fitted within the limits of this deliberately brief treatise.

It is assumed that every judge who takes a serious view of his responsibility will research the subject in much greater depth, especially if he regards dressage as an art rather than just as a variant of equestrian sport.

But we should not overlook the fact that the general standard of riding of a nation will always be judged according to the level of excellence of the best of its riders.

A rider will only remain at the top in dressage if the performance of the rider-horse combination clearly reflects the knowledge and skill of the one who holds the reins.

There is no doubt at all that each and every judgment of a test has some influence on the building up of a riding personality.

I have already mentioned two of the most important factors of valid judging, namely:

— *the objectivity of the judge and*
— *his technical experience and knowledge.*

There is a third factor which is:
— *adeptness at developing the art of scoring* and making *valuable, significant remarks in the inhibiting frame of the prescribed form of test sheet.*

Pirouette rechts auf einem Circul von Laenge des Pferds.
La Pirouette à la droite sur un Circle la longueur du cheval.

In the *Pirouette*, the horse throws its forehand
around a small circle with its hindquarters
remaining in one place. It is a convenient
movement for an Officer leading troops.

115

There is little point in enumerating the advantages and disadvantages of the various different methods that have been tried for overcoming the inadequacies of the system of judging. One can only say, without exaggerating, that from the inception of the FEI tests every attempt has been made to find a method that would completely satisfy the requirements of justness and objectivity and that all methods tried have failed to achieve this object.

At one time or another every one of us has been put by the current system in a quandary that has made him sigh with discouragement or even shout for change.

For one thing, riders and judges have never been able to agree on their preference for one of two methods of ranking performances:

(1) Separate marking and adding up of the marks awarded by each isolated judge. Or,
(2) Deliberation by the assembled judges and concerted marking.

Either method has advantages and disadvantages; but the most important thing is too often overlooked and that is the impression made on the spectator who is always going to be influenced by the score in his appreciation of the good or not so good in dressage.

The most persuasive powers of the most convinced proponent of either method have failed to shake the opinion of the other side, and I certainly do not want to be shot for defending one or the other view.

I will therefore just cite some of the arguments.

The isolation of the individual judges is considered by many to be the best way of arriving at a clear-cut sporting result since each judge is obliged to make a positive decision without deferring to the judgment of another.

If one assumes a broad unity of view amongst judges and equality of expertise, this method has much to recommend it. Insignificant differences of perception can be accepted.

However, wide discrepancies between individual appreciations, which could be explained by the relative ignorance of one or another member of the panel, are very unfair to the competitors and can unjustifiably shake their belief in the rightness of their training method.

The added collective marks of the five judges will very insignificantly correct the result of discrepancy between the marks given for the prescribed movements. If there are only three judges the correcting effect of the collective marks will be nil.

I have already said that some discrepancies are possible for a number of reasons, and especially when the panel consists of judges from different nations with different strongly held opinions on methods of training.

But disconcertingly wide disparities are not unusual in competitions at national level either.

In these cases, it would be a great advantage if judges were assembled, could discuss points of dissent and decide on a concerted judgment. However this would have to be done at the end of each individual presentation and would be very time consuming.

Nevertheless this frequently advocated "consultation" should not be condemned out of hand and completely excluded.

It can be dispensed with if the senior judge mostly agrees with the views of his colleagues on the technical

Cariera an der Wand gerade aus.
La Carriere à la Muraille sur la ligne.

The *Full Gallop* is necessary for an Officer when
he is pursued by the enemy, or when following
a fleeing adversary. It is also good for hunters
who will be safer rides if taught
to gallop properly.

118

merits of a presentation, but take place if this is not the case; differences of opinion could then be noted in the one test sheet. The procedure would protect truly competent judges against imputations of unfitness or bias; more importantly, it would ensure that riders are informed of the reason for dissension among judges and would enable them to choose for consideration the views of the more expert judges.

Thus a judge who found himself frequently out of tune with his colleagues would be obliged to explain and defend his eccentricity and would then either have to decide to dedicate himself more wholeheartedly to the acquisition of knowledge, or have to realize – though perhaps slowly – that he ought to bow out of the company of the experts with as much grace as possible; if he did neither, at least his reputation for incompetence would spread more quickly than it generally does.

Different ideas about training methods have frequently existed and have been tolerated, provided that they were not outrageously aberrant.

A judge should not be castigated for holding firmly to a sincere personal conception of correctness. *But there are some who peddle their (pseudo) knowledge too dearly for the good repute of the whole judging establishment and they ought to be pilloried.*

Presented with unaccountable discrepancies of marks, how can a rider discover which is the pertinent judgment that will help him to remedy his weaknesses and those of his horse?

"Concerted judging" would be of considerable advantage to competitors in all tests of novice, elementary and medium standard.

The idea that separate judging is more com-

Crouppade gerade vor sich.
La Croupade tout droit

The *Croupade* is very good for teaching the
rider a firm seat.

plimentary to judges is largely held but mostly by riders and organizers of competitions; it is not entirely well-founded. To start with the notion itself shows a misunderstanding of the function of a judge and of the significance of the tests.

One valuable objection to separate judging can be made on the ground that it favours impulsive, i.e. insufficiently considered appreciation of performance.

On the other hand it is maintained that separate judging obviates dictatorship of the old (not in years of age but in years of experience).

In the case of conflict of view between two judges of unequal status, it would surely be to the advantage of the riders if the issue were settled by a dictatorial senior judge who can be presumed to possess more knowledge and experience than his junior.

If on the other hand two judges of equal seniority were of a different opinion, diplomacy would be needed to decide which one of the two was most likely to be right. *Eventually of course, in concerted judging, all the various individual perceptions have to be harmonized to produce a hopefully correct concordant judgment – and a common test sheet. In the end it is the test sheet that reflects the conjoined personality of the panel, the dedication of the judges, their objectivity, their technical knowledge, their expertise, and finally the extent of their experience of judging.*

Adeptness at dictating meaningful remarks is another important condition of competence to judge dressage; it is not the strong point of some judges despite their undeniable knowledge.

In fairness to the riders this is an aspect of judging that must be taken seriously.

Calculations of points is the only practical manner

Ballotade auf der Volte rechts.
La Balotade sur la Volte.

If a horse is agile in the *Ballotade*, it will be far
easier and safer for it to jump ditches.

of ranking competitors, especially in novice and elementary tests with a usually big field of starters. But if dressage tests are considered – as they were originally intended to be – a means of helping riders to improve their horsemanship, a judge must learn to express himself clearly in a few meaningful words.

He will never therefore agree to judge a competition without studying the tests beforehand.

He must be perfectly aware of the criteria of correctness of the movements that he is going to have to judge and also completely familiar with the terms that accurately define the quality of a performance. The perfectly apt remark is often elusive except for those who have had a very long practice of judging, but a wrong impression can be conveyed by the badly worded expression of an accurate observation.

The use of incorrect or confusing formulas is not only unfair to the rider; it can also jeopardize the judge's good repute.

Exactness is not all that matters; the influence of a judge has to be constructive and therefore he must not fail to commend what is good as much as condemn what is wrong.

The points should of course be the natural consequence of the remarks.

Since the scale of marks is 10 to 0, it would be normal and logical, whenever there are twenty or more starters, for several competitors to score the same number of points; unfortunately this would displease the organizers and the competitors alike.

They want the judges to rank the competitors, even if this means evaluating differently two or more performances of equal merit.

So the test sheet is divided into almost as many items to be marked as there are lines in an exercise book.

123

Halbe Capriole oder Palso é salto gerade aus.
La demie Capriole tout droit.

The *Half Capriole* is good in cases of emergency,
enabling one to jump across hedges
and other barriers.

There are too many relatively unimportant details to look out for and therefore not enough time to consider really important things. This favours impulsive judging and pernickety fault finding.

Still we ought to remember that in all tests, except those of very advanced standard, the main duty of the judge is to help the riders to put right certain weaknesses and deficiencies of their training programme. The rider benefits very little from a remark to the effect that a rein-back was one step short or a halt not exactly on the prescribed spot. He would like to understand why his horse fights the bit, why the regularity of the beat is upset in the extended gaits, why the transitions lack fluentness and in some way the judge's remarks must give him the answer.

But points do not help to distinguish between important weaknesses of training and relatively insignificant inaccuracies of execution and the result is that the latter have too much influence on the final result.

A number of judges therefore mark inaccuracies in the column for the points, and explain weaknesses attributable to training in the column for remarks, reckoning them in points in the "collective marks" to produce the final result.

It would be impertinent to set down here a prototype of a good test sheet. Every judge must develop for himself a system of marking that is fair and helpful.

The important thing as I have said is to be well prepared. It would be very irresponsible to accept the honour of judging dressage at any venue without having seriously studied the test sheet and the vocabulary of dressage. Young, ambitious judges must resist the temptation to use unconventional terms unless they thoroughly understand their meaning and possible

Spanischer Schritt oder Passagiren gerade aus.
Le Passager sur la ligne.

The horse trained to the *Passage* or *Spanish
Step* will be used by an important person,
a Lord for example, to make an
impressive entrance.

implications. A bloomer is always remembered and sticks to a judge's reputation like an indelible stain on one's ceremonial clothing.

In this matter as in all others, the best guarantee of unimpeachable judging is serious study.

For the purpose of developing greater articulateness, it is good practise to read a familiar test sheet and consider carefully the remarks one could make with regard to each item.

Every presentation starts with an entrance and a salute to the judge. At this stage one has to avoid complicating the issue by deciding whether the horse was sufficiently straight or sufficiently relaxed in the approach; there are not enough strides of the trot or the canter, not enough time either to pass a reliable judgment. A certain amount of abnormal tension is understandable at the beginning of a test, especially in the case of the horse, and should be forgiven. The important thing is "obedience".

Hypercritical consideration of the entrance and the halt can have a negative influence on one's perception of the rest of the presentation.

The judge must always recognize achievement, be it only modest, and expect that the rider and the horse are going to do their best to give a pleasing presentation.

Instead of carefully examining every single step, one should try to obtain an overall picture of horse and rider and assess especially the harmony of purpose existing between the two. Strong points or weak ones can be measured only with regard to this harmony; it wholly determines the quality of a presentation.

A careful counting of inaccuracies is contrary to the object of dressage judging; it prevents a correct

Sanfte Capriole gerade vor sich.
La Capriole entière sur la ligne.

The full Capriole teaches the horse to jump
anything it is pointed at. Purposeful jumping
like this has saved many a brave
officer's life.

estimation of the natural advantages of the horse on the one hand and, on the other hand, of the extent of knowledge, intelligence and skill that the rider has applied in the training of an animal of frequently less than ideal conformation and disposition.

The interests of the rider are best served if one limits the remarks to comments on the quality of each gait, the neatness of the transitions and above all the correctness of the rider's seat and aids.

If a rider has not succeeded in training a horse to associate the activity of its trunk muscles with the activity of its limbs, to come up to his hand and accept the bit correctly, to flex the poll to a degree commensurate with its stated stage of education, to preserve its equilibrium and therefore a regular beat on a perceptibly light tension of the reins, and to respond willingly in all circumstances to discreet aids, weaknesses in all or any of these respects will be continually evidenced throughout the test, whether on straight lines or curved ones, in turns, half-halts and movements on two tracks. The judge can then spare himself the effort to remark upon those deficiencies time after time.

If he believes, as he ought to, that it is his duty to guide the rider along the right course, he will use the column for remarks to point out the root cause of the failings.

A profusion of criticisms obscures the significance of the judgment and leaves the rider baffled as how best to remedy his weaknesses.

One could say, for example: "A horse with favourable aptitudes but insufficiently developed submissiveness (as evidenced in the half-halts and the rein-back)"; or "in the extended movements, steps

Das Pferd zum Fahnen zu gewöhnen.
Accoutumer le cheval au drapeau.

It is necessary for the horses of Officers and keen
riders to get used to flags so they will not
shy away.

quickened rather than lengthened because of the insufficient engagement of the hind legs"; or again "inadequate responsiveness to the aids manifested by the obtrusive but ineffectual actions of the rider". This sort of remark gives the rider the assistance that he seeks (assuming of course that he admits the judge's superior wisdom and welcomes constructive criticism).

The judge may be a little undecided in his estimation of the entrance, halt and salute, but immobility during the salute and the subsequent transition are easy to observe and to mark. Now if the horse shuffles, it is almost entirely due to a sudden flagging of the rider's energy. This ought to be pointed out but few judges ever bother to do so.

There is of course very little room for remarks if official printed sheets have to be used. Hence if a judge has to make a remark he has to do so in as few words as possible. He must therefore have at his command a vocabulary of significant terms. They are all contained in the vast literature devoted to classical horsemanship but one must be aware of the fact that some authors of the past have used the same term to define completely different things. To avoid misunderstanding it is absolutely necessary to know and accept the definitions prescribed in the dressage rules of the FEI. Within those limits, it should be possible to develop a sufficiently expressive vocabulary. One must avoid in any case highfaluting or idiosyncratic terms; their use is never a proof of superiority as a judge. The important thing is to have at one's complete command the limited vocabulary of conventional terms and of using the appropriate one in each situation.

Very expert horsemen have written books that are of limited value nowadays only because undoubtedly

Das Pferd Schüß freÿ zü machen.
Le cheval d'arquebusade

Training the horse to become used to the rider
shooting from his back serves to assist the
soldier and the hunter.

132

excellent notions are expressed in original terms that meant something to the author but are mysterious for most readers. And so if judges of dressage want to talk clearly to riders, they must avoid the pitfalls of sophistication.

Before concluding this little primer for dressage judges, I have a few more words to say.

Mastery of the art of horsemanship is never purely the result of good "schooling". One can inspire a rider to develop his natural talent, but finally it is he who must put in the hard work that is always required to achieve proficiency. The same can be said of mastery of the art of judging.

Courses can be organized for judges, opportunities for learning provided, too often with the end result of producing only more or less efficient "fault finders". But the "true blue" judge is entirely a man of his own making.

Quick fault finding and self-confidence can be acquired by the extensive practice of judging, but is this really in the spirit of dressage judging?

Good dressage judging is very difficult but it can be a fascinating pursuit.

Let us not forget that the future of good horsemanship lies to a very considerable extent in the hands of dressage judges. Enthusiastic practitioners of the art must be encouraged instead of being constantly disheartened by the quibbles of spineless judges.

Das Pferd zur Trommel zu gewöhnen.
Accoutumer le cheval au Tambour.

It is important to get horses used to the noise of
drums to prepare them for the tumult
of battle.